"I've been waiting for Randy's book for years. Here we have the broken heart and quick mind of an urban practitioner-scholar, calling God's people to believe they can embrace the urban poor for Christ. His journey and that of his family are really an 'every-believer' model. We can all do a part of this, even if not the whole. Thank you, Randy."

LON ALLISON, DIRECTOR, BILLY GRAHAM CENTER, WHEATON COLLEGE

"An unforgettable trip to real life in Fresno to see how Jesus uses real people to make a real difference. Essential reading for anyone who wants to see God's dreams come true in the city. Randy compellingly weaves stories from the streets with stories from the gospel and provides insightful guidelines for those who want to discover how God might want to use their mustard seeds in the city."

TOM SINE, FOUNDER AND DIRECTOR, MUSTARD SEED ASSOCIATES, AND AUTHOR OF *JOINING GOD'S CONSPIRACY* AND *LIVING ON PURPOSE*

"What a wonderful book. Many people are talking about transformation these days; Randy White shows us what it looks like with his roots planted in the soil of his neighborhood. This kind of transformation removes the distance between object and subject as it changes both partners. I am already making plans to use this in my teaching."

JUDE TIERSMA WATSON, TEAM DIRECTOR, LA INNERCHANGE, AND ASSOCIATE PROFESSOR OF URBAN MISSION, FULLER THEOLOGICAL SEMINARY

"Randy White takes us on a mind-opening journey once again, this time onto the challenging and transformative pathway of discipleship in the context of the city. Based on his years of living in and studying the urban context, White distills in a manner not found in any other book I know the power of the written text in understanding his own transformation, even as he facilitates and nurtures a similar transformation among young adults and others seeking to appreciate and encounter God in the complex and often chaotic sociocultural landscape of the city. This book would interest anyone who is grappling with the question of what it means to be a disciple of Christ in our world today. *Encounter God in the City* is a must-have book in particular for those who are responsible for mentoring or leading others into a full embrace of and by God. White does us all a great service by not only sharing his story but providing tangible examples and tools for transformation."

MICHAEL A. MATA, NATIONAL DIRECTOR, TOOLS FOR TRANSFORMATION, WORLD VISION, U.S.

"*Encounter God in the City* is a road map to becoming an apostle at the intersection of love, pain and hope. Randy White has captured the bittersweet beauty of mutual transformation that comes in serving. Years of experience living among those he serves invest his words with power and give his insights an incisive edge, cutting to the quick of urban dysfunction. This book is both uplifting and hands-on practical—a must-read for anyone who wants to live out their faith authentically."
BARBARA J. ELLIOTT, AUTHOR OF *STREET SAINTS: RENEWING AMERICA'S CITIES*, AND FOUNDER OF THE CENTER FOR RENEWAL, HOUSTON, TEXAS

"There is a redemptive art to urban ministry. It is the art of storytelling—taking the mistold tale of human existence and retelling the story from the perspective of the love of God. Anyone desirous of seeing this redemptive art in practice should read *Encounter God in the City*. This book is a must read for theological faculty in our seminaries. It is a how-to manual in contextual theology and experiential education. It is a must read for practitioners of ministry in the city who are serious about learning how to be agents of transformation, and a must read for all Christians who are not afraid of being surprised by a joy that calls them to holistic ministry in an urban world. It has become a must read for all of our students."
DAVE FRENCHAK, PRESIDENT, SEMINARY CONSORTIUM FOR URBAN PASTORAL EDUCATION (SCUPE)

"Randy White takes us to the mean streets of urban America and uncovers there treasures of the kingdom hidden from the natural eye. Years of firsthand experience living in the 'hood give him rare insights into the surprising ways God can be discovered among the disenfranchised of the city. In candid, sometimes painful self-disclosure, he invites us to look into the unlovely faces of the broken and catch glimpses of the mystery of the Christ who said 'inasmuch as you have done it unto (cared for) the least of these you have done it unto me.'"
BOB LUPTON, URBAN COMMUNITY DEVELOPER, AUTHOR OF *THEIRS IS THE KINGDOM* AND *RENEWING THE CITY*

"Urban ministry has a strange, fleeting glamour that draws lots of outsiders for lots of different reasons but seldom holds them long. The ones who stay do not romanticize the poverty which surrounds them, but they do come to love it—the way Randy White loves it—for the many ways it reveals their own poverty. What Randy has learned better than most, however, is to also love his neighbors' strength and goodness, and to allow them to make him a better man. In these vital, practical, inspirational pages, he shows the rest of us that most excellent way."
BART CAMPOLO, FOUNDER AND CHAPLAIN, MISSION YEAR

ENCOUNTER GOD IN THE CITY

Onramps to Personal and
Community Transformation

Randy White

Foreword by Ray Bakke

IVP Books

An imprint of InterVarsity Press
Downers Grove, Illinois

InterVarsity Press
P.O. Box 1400, Downers Grove, IL 60515-1426
World Wide Web: www.ivpress.com
E-mail: mail@ivpress.com

InterVarsity Press® is the book-publishing division of InterVarsity Christian Fellowship/USA®, a student movement active on campus at hundreds of universities, colleges and schools of nursing in the United States of America, and a member movement of the International Fellowship of Evangelical Students. For information about local and regional activities, write Public Relations Dept., InterVarsity Christian Fellowship/USA, 6400 Schroeder Rd., P.O. Box 7895, Madison, WI 53707-7895, or visit the IVCF website at <www.intervarsity.org>.

Scripture quotations, unless otherwise noted, are from the New Revised Standard Version of the Bible, copyright 1989 by the Division of Christian Education of the National Council of the Churches of Christ in the USA. Used by permission. All rights reserved.

The edition of the chart on page 139 is from Cross-Cultural Connections by Duane H. Elmer. Copyright ©2002 by Duane H. Elmer. Used with permission of InterVarsity Press, P.O. Box 1400, Downers Grove, IL 60515. www.ivpress.com

Design: Cindy Kiple
Images: Tiffany Cable

ISBN-10: 0-8308-3389-7
ISBN-13: 978-0-8308-3389-4

Printed in the United States of America ∞

Library of Congress Cataloging-in-Publication Data

White, Randy, 1956-
  Encounter God in the city: on ramps to personal and community
  transformation / Randy White.
      p. cm.
  Includes bibliographical references.
  ISBN-13: 978-0-8308-3389-4 (pbk.: alk. paper)
  ISBN-10: 0-8308-3389-7 (pbk.: alk. paper)
  1. City missions. 2. Cities and towns—Religious
  aspects—Christianity. 3. City churches. I. Title.
  BV2653.W45 2006
  253.09173'2—dc22

                                                          2006013027

P	18	17	16	15	14	13	12	11	10	9	8	7	6	5	4	3	2	1
Y	21	20	19	18	17	16	15	14	13	12	11	10	09	08	07	06			

To my sons,

Joseph and Jameson,

who

Stand tall like skyscrapers

Span gaps like bridges

Sow the seeds of shalom

In the fertile crevices of

Broken streets and

Unlikely saints

Contents

PART 3—ONRAMPS AND SPEED BUMPS: *Steering Toward Transformation of the City*

Foreword

For those of us who accept Randy White's invitation to experience God's "lab of the Spirit," it means taking the offramp to the little community of Lowell in downtown Fresno, California, where Randy and Tina White have lived for a little less than 1 percent of all history since Christ. This is where Randy has been going to school.

Many years ago the assistant superintendent of the Seattle public schools told me that, in choosing between competing applicants for school principal positions, it is critical to discern the difference between the person who has twenty years of experience and the person who has one experience twenty times. Randy epitomizes the gift of acting, reflecting and then learning from experience. His neighbors are his teachers and this book models what we might call "mission in reverse." The community is teacher; he is the learner.

When the Russian missionaries came to Alaska in the eighteenth century, they noticed that when the Eskimos or Aleut villagers were able to kill a whale or large animals, they ate, of course, but placed some of the meat, bone and blood down in the water as a sacrifice to the god who had shown mercy to them by making these giant animals sacrifice their own lives to keep these vulnerable people alive generation after generation. The Russian missionaries documented the fact that the Holy Spirit was there long before they got there, teaching the people the doctrine of sacrifice and other important truths. The missionaries' new message was "we know the name of this God." He visited us once. His name is Jesus. The gospel spread like wildfire over Alaska as a result. Michael Oleksa documents that in his book *Orthodox Alaska: A Theology of Mission*.

Like those Russian missionaries of old, Randy knows that the Spirit of God was active in the inner city long before he and Tina got there. He sees assets and builds on them. Of all the people he introduced me to in this book, the one I think I'll never forget is a little waiflike girl with the name Eternity, who frankly smelled like hell while doing crafts with twenty other kids around their dining room table. The Whites know what incarnation means: to live vulnerably while hungering for righteousness and seeking shalom, the justice and peace of God.

This book brought back memories. My Napoleon—the teen in the Fresno gang, with the surprising interest in international politics and our nation's China policy—was my Chicago gang neighbor Jim Lane, the leader of our neighborhood gang called TJO. I found him in a bookstore reading on China. Jim had committed a felony to gain his exemption from the draft and the Vietnam War. He lived in our home for a while.

Between the onramps and the speed bumps, the neighborhood has taken the stained glass off Scripture. It turns out to be a dialogue between Isaiah or Paul and a living, changing community. I remember we used to have Bible quizzes we called "sword drills," but I don't ever recall "smashing giant cockroaches" with my big, black Bible like Randy did. It may horrify some to think the Bible can be put to such use, but it is no surprise to me.

It struck me as I read this book that Randy has a lot in common with Vincent Donovan, who wrote of his seventeen-year safari among the Masai tribal communities in Kenya in his book *Christianity Redis-covered*. Donovan writes that "every theology or theory must be based on previous missionary experience, and that any theory or theology which is not based on previous experience is empty words, of use to no one."[1] Like Donovan, Randy does not see the planting of the church as the chief goal of his mission. Churches are, in fact, signs of and agents for the kingdom of God—which is a set of values and a view of reality that comes from Jesus and Scripture. This book is not about strategies and programs for churches to "take our cities." In the spirit of the incarnation, it is about being present in a community and living in a human scale relationship to the people and systems that impact people in the city.

I know Randy as a scholar with a doctorate, but I also know him as a poet with sensitivities I could only imagine. I perceive that there is a growing gulf in the church today between the "mission and purpose-driven" forms of Christianity, and those for whom the incarnation of Jesus is both message and model. Jesus chose twelve "that they might be *with* him," according to Mark 3:14 (NIV, emphasis mine). My sense is that Jesus spent 50 percent of his working three years with twelve people, precisely because he believed that discipleship is something to be taught and something to be caught. When I read Randy's stories of encounters over so many years, I don't hear him strategizing for InterVarsity or laying down bold tracks for students in mission. I hear a compelling call to an urban community: Come and be with Jesus Christ, in relationship to these broken and troubled neighbors. It's not rocket science with Randy; it sounds more like the psalmist who wrote: "Blessed be the LORD, / for he has wondrously shown his steadfast love to me / when I was beset as a city under seige" (Ps 31:21).

Ray Bakke
Founder, International Urban Associates

Acknowledgments

People say that couples who have been married for many years begin to sound like each other, even look like each other. (Not good news for my wife, by the way.) They complete each other's sentences. They adopt each other's language and posture. Again, I get the better end of the deal, as Tina's words are always more gracious than mine; I absorb her quiet rhythms. The lessons of this book are ours.

Specific authors and leaders have had a similar effect on me. Their profound and original thinking has seeped into my mind; their examples of ministry in the city saturate my life. They have become a part of me. I owe a great debt, a fact that will be obvious to anyone reading this book.

Ray Bakke is one of those. His love of the city and of history, theology and art has been contagious; I have been infected for more than a decade. I am grateful for his fresh and creative lens on Scripture and for his invitation to accompany him to experience firsthand the new global city on several continents. John Perkins, Father Ben Beltran, Chris Rice, Melba Maggay, Jim Westgate and H. Spees have all shaped the way I think and act. Their words, beliefs and values echo throughout this book.

I am deeply grateful for Scott Bessenecker, director of InterVarsity's Global Projects, for his partnership in the gospel to equip "new friars"—

young, emerging influencers for transformational service among the world's poor—as well as for his leadership in the Experiential Discipleship Taskforce, where much of my thinking for this book was catalyzed. I prize his patient friendship—and the privilege of watching each other get sick in alternating countries.

I can't imagine the void that would be left without my connection to the missional community of Fresno, including friends at One by One Leadership, ESA/Love Inc., the Downtown Pastors Cluster, No Name Fellowship, dozens of agencies and churches that take the city seriously, and of course, all those who have moved intentionally into the most traumatized neighborhoods of the city—especially those unnamed saints in Lowell—to seek and embody shalom.

I am indebted to InterVarsity urban project directors in more than two dozen cities across the United States who have invited me to serve in their projects in some capacity over the past decade, and for those who contributed urban project formats to the supplemental online appendixes, including Barb Weidman, Todd Minturn, Wanda Classen and Jenn Vettrus.

Many people contributed helpful comments, corrections and criticisms to the manuscript, including Miriam Adeney, Beth Eckloff, Heidi and Joe White, Seth and Hanna Gravette, Scott Bessenecker, Josh Harper, Jameson White, Tiffany Cable (who, as an artist and relocator, also painted the cover art and lives what she paints), Betty Hidgon, my editor Al Hsu, and several anonymous readers. Jim Tebbe, InterVarsity's director of missions and the Urbana Student Mission Convention, encouraged this project. And thanks to my sons, Joseph and Jameson, who provided suggestions and egged me on with "Ya done yet?!" With all that help, I can safely say all remaining mistakes or shortcomings are mine.

Introduction

Ever notice how there's a spectacular nature scene on the cover of just about every devotional guide or Bible study book: a thundering waterfall, a golden sunset, a snow-peaked mountain? There's never a graffiti-covered wall, a cyclone fence with laundry hanging on it, the faces of inner-city kids or the familiar tangle of concrete onramps and offramps. How could *those* things have anything to do with the soaring and magnificent themes of faith and the sovereignty of God? Judging from the cover of my quiet-time guide, if I want to commune with God, I apparently need a rainbow or a river to inspire me. Rail depots and rusty rebar just won't do the trick. Yet many fine scholars have acknowledged that the Bible identifies *cities* as a key focus of God's attention.

This is a book about the exceptional power of experience in the city to act as an onramp leading onto the highway of transformation for both the disciple and the city. I have had the privilege of seeing this power firsthand in fifteen years of ministry in the city, in a decade of choreographing experiential discipleship projects in United States cities and in observing or participating in ministries in megacities on several continents. Experiential discipleship projects are events that engage participants in service and learning in a way that employs a cycle of action, reflection and whole-life application.

Because this book arises out of the storehouse of transformational experiences, I make no apologies for its first-person perspective. On the contrary, that perspective is the very essence and point of my message. My experiences as a follower of Jesus living intentionally in a high-crime, high-poverty neighborhood and the experiences of others who have made similar choices have convinced me that the interplay of experience, reflection and whole-life application, when lived out in the context of the city, produces a degree of transformation unparalleled by any other context.

But the stories in this book embody more than mere experiences alone. They have happened *spontaneously* (serendipitously— orchestrated by God) or were *directed* (planned—orchestrated by leaders). They have then been leveraged for maximum impact on my life in Christ and for maximum insight into the city through reflection and application. These stories uniquely demonstrate three things: First, they show the power of experience to reveal a person's true self and those things that most need to be transformed. Part one of this book focuses on how experiential discipleship in the city remakes us and creates new onramps for our growth and development. The stories in it reveal the sometimes-invisible forces that shape the lives of those who are caught in the crush of urban poverty. In part two we will look at some of those forces, examining the power of experience to uncloak what is hidden. The stories in it reveal the strategic power of experience to mobilize God's people for transformational influence in the city. In part three we will look closely at transformation itself, examine barriers to it, and outline proactive steps that individuals and groups can take in their city. A leader's guide about how to design and implement experiential discipleship events in a city is available online at ivpress.com.

Why focus on the city? The whole world is moving to cities.[1] Already, more than 50 percent of the earth's people—and 62 percent of all Christians—live in cities.[2] In the next twenty years "more than one-quarter of the world's population will be poor and living in the squatter settlements of the developing world."[3] In the United States, more than half of the population now lives in just forty cities of a million or more people. In the past twenty-five years Las Vegas exploded with 250-percent population growth, while Houston grew by 140 percent.[4] Cities are magnets pulling the hopeful across any barrier, and they endure any hardship. They are twenty-four-hour-a-day catch basins for the vulnerable. But some cities are losing population as old industries die. We are in the beginning phases of the most massive migration, both in and out of cities, the world has ever known. And it is ramping up.

Why focus on the city? Today's cities, even more than nation-states, influence economic systems, political alliances and social movements. This makes cities a strategic investment: what influences the city influences the world. The city needs a growing cadre of young leaders—both college and graduate students as well as those already in the marketplace—who will link their skills, their privileges and their sense of well-being to the well-being of the city. In today's globalized world, to shape the city is to shape the way people experience life itself.

Why focus on the city? While for some the city is the normal context of faith development, part and parcel of what it means to follow Jesus and the stage where the drama of life before God has unfolded, for many others the city represents a huge question mark. Is it a place where faith can thrive? Is it a place of blessing, or evidence of a curse? Is the city a spiritually fertile place where a person can sustain a vibrant relationship with God?[5] For many whose faith was nurtured in the womb of a gated suburban community or in the calm rhythms of small-town America, there's a lot of doubt about the answer. For decades, that doubt led to the flight away from cities by the white middle class and, even more significantly, by the black middle class as well. Ethnic minorities now comprise 25 percent of new suburban populations.[6] While books on ministry in cities, on community organizing, on urban evangelism or simply on how to serve people in cities abound, there are very few resources that view the city as a place to grow your faith and discover a meaningful life, as a place that transforms you or as a place where your own transformation can have an effect.

And so it's my privilege to share personally and honestly some of what I have learned about myself as a disciple from life in the city, some of what I have learned about the forces shaping the lives of others in the city and some of what I have learned about orchestrating and leveraging experience in the city as a mechanism for transformation. These lessons are onramps to involvement in something larger than us: the story of God's mission. This mission is the highway we are called to be on, a road distinguished by the faith journeys of those whose hearts are set on pilgrimage toward God's shalom kingdom. Of them, the psalmist wrote, "Happy are those whose strength is in you, / in whose heart are the highways to Zion" (Ps 84:5). I hope this book encourages you to take onramps to that highway and even equips you to create a few onramps for others.

One thing I've learned about onramps is that they are not all created equally. Some are long and gentle, with time to pick up speed and merge with the flow. Others shock you alive. One onramp in Los Angeles joins a curving section of the 110 freeway in no more than thirty feet. It was built during a time when cars went forty-five miles per hour. Now they are screaming around that section at seventy-five. Achieving zero to seventy-five in thirty feet seems unreasonable, and so do many experiences I have had in the city. Getting up to speed through those experiences has been God's strategy for transformation in *my* life and, amazingly, in the *city* as well. Talk about win-win.

PART 1

Road Ready

MY OWN

EXTREME OVERHAUL

1

Don't Bother Me.
I'm Teaching on Compassion!

It was dusk in the Devil's Triangle, the neighborhood with the highest crime and poverty rates in Fresno, California. Several months earlier my family and I had relocated to the Triangle (its formal name: The Lowell Community). Fresno has been called the Appalachia of the West and is the number-one city in the nation for concentrated poverty.[1]

We were full of fresh passages from the Bible of God's concern for the city and his love for the poor, full of good intentions for the community and full of hope that we could be part of the solution to its problems. That night, a small group of college students were gathered in our large living room to learn about ministry among those on the margins of society and get some training for the inner-city tutoring program they would be serving in. Some of the students lived with us in that large, ninety-year-old house.

Right in the middle of our in-depth Bible study on Isaiah 58, the classic passage that in so many ways defines discipleship as compassionate action on behalf of the poor, the pounding began. I ignored it at first, wanting to continue the study. After all, the "fasting" God had chosen—welcoming the homeless into your house, supplying food from your pantry, clothing the naked—were all serious commands. But the pounding persisted. I rolled my eyes and told everybody to hold on for a moment.

I opened the front door to a man who looked like a cast member for a zombie movie. He was disheveled and filthy, had glassy eyes and smelled. I was instantly on guard. When I said, "Yes?" he simply handed me a note stating he was deaf, his car had just broken down three blocks up the road, and he needed three dollars for gas.

I rolled my eyes again. Since moving in we had been targeted by a steady stream of transient men who appeared on our doorstep, many of them with similar stories. I had naively wondered what it was about that section of road that caused such car problems. It didn't take long to get wise. The part about being deaf was a nice touch, but this guy looked familiar, and I suspected it was a fabrication. Without hesitation, I handed him back his note and said, "Sorry, I can't help you," and closed the door to his bewildered face.

I walked straight back to the Bible study and resumed teaching about compassionate action on behalf of the poor. But the expressions on the students' faces made it clear that they wanted to talk about what had just happened and about how my actions fit—actually, didn't fit—with what we were studying. The rest of the evening was dedicated to debriefing the experience, trying to come up with how I might have responded better. They asked, "Could you have acted with an intelligent compassion that demonstrated the love of Christ without enabling the man's problems?" They asked, "Should you have at least taken more time with him?" In other words, I became the study, and the hypocrisy of *talking* compassion without *practicing* it was the focus of God's lesson plan by way of the city that night. My extreme overhaul was well underway.

My family and I knew when we moved into the Lowell neighborhood that we would be on a huge learning curve. But we weren't prepared for the urban "chemical peel" that the next several years would bring through our experiences there. Much of what was being stripped away by this Spirit-led overhaul process was ugly, like layers of rust on an ancient city bridge, which has to come off in order to restore the structural integrity and original design. The act of living incarnationally, that is, leaving our "safe" and controlled environment for an unpredictable urban neighborhood, activated for us the mechanisms of repentance. More than a decade later, the experiences in this urban neighborhood are still being leveraged into life changes; the rusty layers of self-protection, of convenience, of materialism and a host of other corrosive qualities are still coming off in our lives.

Transformation happens most powerfully for those who would follow Christ when the *word* of God and the *work* of God are experienced in close proximity to each other. That juxtaposition can be leveraged through *reflection and response* to make the effect of word and work more powerful and permanent. This coupling of experience and biblical reflection, followed by whole-life application and action in a context that includes conflict or tension, has profound effects. These effects have been shown to provide a new dissonance with our prior experiences or assumptions.[2] The result of that dissonance is the construction of a new onramp to our growth in Christ.

Scott Bessenecker, director of InterVarsity's Global Projects and Global Urban Trek, calls this *dissonance learning* leading to an *experiential discipleship*. Discipleship is the process of learning from Jesus. In fact, the very word *disciple* literally means "learner." According to the authors of *Developing Leaders for Urban Ministries,* "A disciple is a follower who learns to be like the one he/she follows (Luke 6:40)."[3] As author Brian McLaren points out, disciples are like apprentices,[4] walking alongside their teachers, absorbing every aspect of who they are, what they know and how they do what they do. The learning of the first disciples was different from what is often acquired in Western settings, where the mere transfer of information seems to be the goal and the storage and retrieval of data is the proof of success. Educational researcher Jack Mezirow has demonstrated that learning is a series of transformations in the way we make meaning in our lives.[5] It is a transformation of the cues in our lives that tell us what is important. The learning of the disciples included following, a life posture that led to transformation. They were transformed to become more like Christ in his values, purposes and methods. Obviously such learning influences the disciple, but it also influences the circumstances and people around him or her. The role of *experience* in this process, and in particular, experience that is uniquely generated by participation in transformational ministry in the city, is the focus of this book.

2

Disorientation and Discovery

KUNDARA AND PETER

We were middle class and white, joining a community that was mostly made up of migrant farm workers, Southeast Asian refugees, a chaotic youth population heavily into gangs and a small, cynical, fearful population of elderly homeowners who were just hanging on. Our education, our clothing, our car, our language, our family rhythms—all separated us, made us stand out in ways we didn't even want to acknowledge. The automatic outcome was a newly reflective posture in our lives. Even the smallest incidents became fertile ground for thought and a new perspective. The experience of realizing how different we were became an onramp to God remaking us.

During our first year in the neighborhood, we hosted rehearsals in our living room for a preteen girls choir that a local ministry had put together, made up almost entirely of refugee children from Laos and Cambodia. One afternoon, one of the girls came a little early for practice. Kundara sat at the piano in my living room, plunking absently at the keys. Her back was to me, and I noticed her studying the room as she waited for the rest of the girls to arrive. After only thirty seconds, she turned to me and said, "Pastor Randy, you're rich aren't you?" Everything in me wanted to protest. I nearly yelled, "Are you kidding?" I wanted to say, "Honey, rich people don't move to this neighborhood." I wanted to say, "You don't understand; I'm on a ministry salary." But I looked at her bare feet. It was winter. I remembered that her parents had to swim across the Mekong River to escape with their lives. I recalled that she was born in the Wat Tham Krabok refugee camp in Thailand, where they had lived in limbo for years. And now her family and another large family were crammed into a two-room apartment in my neighborhood. The only answer that had any integrity was "Yes, I guess I am," but I found myself adding, "and I try to use what I have for God."

Ever since that experience, which has been reinforced by almost identical conversations with other children and adults here, it has been difficult to deny my relative wealth and justify my spotty record of stewarding it. The verses in the Bible about stewardship of wealth and the Bible's surprising and frequent emphasis on money and its power to displace God began to jump out at me. When placed in proximity to Kundara's bare feet, these Scriptures pressed themselves indelibly on my mind. They forced me to admit how self-justifying I was, and it became easier for me to acknowledge my privileges. This increased my compassion. The link that reflection played in bridging what I *knew* to what I *did* was profound.[1] Another layer was stripped away in the process of refinishing my soul.

PETER UPSIDE DOWN

This kind of revelation is often the outcome of God-orchestrated experiences. Those experiences become transformational when they are followed by reflection, action and whole-life application. We see this happening all the time in the Bible. The apostle Peter's heady experience on a rooftop in the city, which led to the reshaping of his perspective, illustrates some key components of experiential discipleship.

Peter's vision of the world had been nurtured by the ethnocentrism of his culture and a strict interpretation of Jewish ritual law. He saw himself as "clean" according to Jewish custom and certain other people as "unclean" according to that same custom. So, when the Lord commanded him in a rooftop vision to eat things that were unclean according to his tradition, this presented what Mezirow calls a *disorienting dilemma.*[2] "How can you ask me to do that?" he responded. Clearly God was setting the stage for a tangible lesson in human dignity, because soon after, an envoy of the Gentile soldier Cornelius arrived at the place where Peter was staying to invite him to his home. As a Gentile, not to mention a representative of the occupying force, Cornelius was unclean to Peter. Nevertheless, Peter provided Cornelius's delegation with hospitality and then took the *action* of following them to Cornelius's home.

What were his thoughts as he stood in the home of a Gentile, with other Gentiles pressed closely around, listening to Cornelius's summary of the work of God in his life? Peter went on to share an open *reflection* on the work of God in his own life, how God had confronted him about what is or isn't "clean." He revealed that he had shifted in his thinking and had come to understand in practical terms that God shows no partiality.

When the Holy Spirit fell on the whole assembly, it sent Peter into a second round of *reflection* as he considered not only the spiritual interest of the Gentiles, but also the obvious fact that they were as eligible for salvation as he was (Acts 10:45). Peter took the *action* of baptizing this household, then stayed for several days in the home of these people who had formerly been regarded by him as unclean (v. 48). On his return to the city of Jerusalem Peter *applied* his new insights as he advocated for the validity of the conversion of the Gentiles before the leaders in Jerusalem, and he reiterated his revelation that they were to make no distinction between Jews and Gentiles (Acts 11:12).

KEY ELEMENTS, KEY RESULTS

This story demonstrates the key elements in any experiential discipleship cycle. We see the *word* of God expressed to Peter, followed by a *disorienting dilemma*. Then Peter took corresponding *actions*, which were followed by more *experiences*. These led to *reflection*, followed by *application*. This is God's methodology for getting a disciple onto the highway of his values, his vision of the world, and for revealing what it will take to advance God's kingdom.

Kundara's bare-footed observation and Peter's upsetting rooftop vision in the context of the city are experiences that act as signs indicating the onramp is coming soon. They say to followers of Christ, "Get ready to merge onto a different road." For Peter, the sign was a sheet full of animals. For me, it was Kundara's bare feet in winter and her observations about my privileges. It changed the way I thought about myself. It continues to prevent me from lying to myself about my relative wealth.

3

Sandpaper Surprises and Reflective Learning

NAPOLEON

I know how Peter must have felt after his vision on the rooftop. Deeply held prejudices and fears are often shaped over time, and therefore time is required to dismantle them. But sometimes God uses a gentle sanding to remove a portion of the soul's covering that is dead.

It was like that when I met Napoleon, a stocky seventeen-year-old who reminded me of a modern-day conqueror, though he was only in high school. The sides of his head were shaved close and the black hair on the top was slicked back into a short ponytail. His very baggy clothes were immaculately pressed.

Whenever he entered my house, Napoleon took the red gang bandanna off his belt and folded it neatly away into his back pocket. His sharp mind became apparent in conversation, but we came from different worlds and we both knew it. We went out for pie on Wednesdays for a while, and I learned that he loved history. He initiated conversation about Alexander the Conqueror's exploits and strategies, about American presidents and political parties, and about how lame school is, except for history. Often, when we returned to my house, he would hang out to read magazines in the living room.

But even though I'd gotten to know Napoleon, I wasn't ready for the series of surprises he threw at me. One night, after an hour of reading *National Geographic,* he put the magazine down and looked at me. His simple, focused question was like a scalpel in the hand of God. He asked, "So, Randy, what you think will happen when Hong Kong reverts to China?" Napoleon wanted to discuss the ramifications: what would it mean for its people, its future and its political system? I was flabbergasted that a teen gang member would be interested in global, geopolitical movements, let alone read about and understand them. I wonder what incredulous look must have been on my face, created by this dissonance, which drew me toward a deeper reflection on my prejudices. Such reflection is now being recognized by many researchers as a normative outcome of dissonance.[1]

On another occasion, Napoleon informed me that his father, who was estranged from the family, had offered to buy him a used car. I assumed this was every high school kid's dream and that Napoleon would jump at the chance. But I marveled in disbelief when, instead, he told me he'd asked his father for a computer. I visited Napoleon on the day he set it up in his living room. The tiny living room in his dilapidated house was barely large enough for his mother, his sisters and his brother, but all of them crowded around Napoleon as he proudly connected the cables and fired it up. The action of standing there with them, seeing their joy, hearing them talk about the possibilities and watching a new world unfold before them created another dissonance for me. More of my assumptions about city kids had been challenged, more of my stereotypes about poor families dismantled, more soul calluses gone.

On yet another occasion, Napoleon showed up at a neighborhood cleanup day. I watched as crew leaders assembled and organized volunteers into teams with leaders. Seven volunteers were sent to stand near Napoleon and wondered aloud about where the leader was. It didn't occur to anyone, myself included, that *he* was to be their leader. As he got his crew going, he slipped by the house of another gang member and roused him from his bed. He would not let him skip out on this day. His crew, composed of gang members and well-meaning white people, successfully completed its mission of planting pansies—and had fun doing it. I called the organizer to discuss how Napoleon had surprised me. But it was no surprise to her. She had spent time with him and had experienced her own awakenings.

HOLY SANDPAPER

With these three experiences, the reflection that followed and later involvement with Napoleon, God was using the city to sand away the sin of low expectations and faulty assumptions that characterized my early attitudes about him. I didn't know him, didn't understand his potential. I only saw his hair, his demeanor, his clothes and his gang bandanna. His remarkable qualities shocked me into what Mezirow calls *reflective learning,* which involves "assessment or reassessment of assumptions . . . [and] becomes transformative whenever assumptions or premises are found to be distorting, inauthentic, or otherwise invalid."[2] It was like losing layers of skin.

Now, ten years later, Napoleon is graduating from college and occasionally preaches at a local church. I can't look at young men from the neighborhood in the same way. Maybe it's not skin that is being removed. Maybe it's cataracts. Now I can see.

Obviously God orchestrates and leverages our experiences anywhere and everywhere. It is God who enables us "to will and to work for his good pleasure" (Phil 2:13). Our lives—no matter what the context: urban or suburban or rural—provide him with the raw material he uses to invite us into a more mature relationship with him and to fashion us to more closely resemble the Lord Jesus. What I have found in the city is a set of circumstances that are so radically different from the "normal" I had wrapped around myself that it's a whole new arena for faith development. This playing field is foreign to me, even after a decade here, and because of that, I am still paying close attention. There seems to be an endless supply of experiences that are ready-made to address the discipleship issues that the Spirit of God wants to take up in my life.

4

Action and Reflection

I AM NOT MR. ROGERS

Sometimes the juxtaposition of events from both inside the neighborhood and outside the neighborhood acts like a twin-blade razor in the hands of God. For example, within one twenty-four-hour period two things happened, one in Lowell and one on the national news, that would forever influence the way I saw kids in my urban neighborhood, and myself: (1) I met Jaleel, and (2) Mr. Rogers died.

Jaleel was a problem from the first moment he came to our home for the tutoring program. He was bouncing off the walls. The college students who were tutoring didn't know how to handle him. We had tried time-outs for him on the carpet. We had dried his tears lovingly. By the time the program ended that day he was in total meltdown; he hadn't had a chance on the computer. He escaped in a fit to the alley.

In my frustration I was tempted to just let him go, but Tiffany, our part-time intern who had relocated to his street, reminded me that Jaleel was only five years old and lived on the other side of the neighborhood. So I self-consciously and carefully carried the screaming and kicking boy back from the corner he had run to. It must have been quite a spectacle, a large, white man first trying to convince, then dragging, then hoisting a struggling black child to his waist, who was all the while crying and screeching, "Help me, help me!" He was riding my hip like an urban cowboy, delivering well-practiced blows to the side of my head, knocking my glasses off and generally looking like someone being kidnapped. I hurried back to the house with him. Part of me was glad this loud event hadn't been noticed. Part of me was disturbed that no one had asked what I was doing.

Jaleel's calm older brother and two of our tutors stuffed him in a car, arms and legs flailing, and drove him home. They pulled him across the street to his house as he shouted, "I want to be run over!" and delivered him to his mother, who thankfully happened to be there on this occasion. I was relieved; problem solved, or at least out of my purview.

WWMRD?

The next day, my head still sore from Jaleel's little fists, I saw an online news report that Mr. Rogers had died. Fred Rogers, an ordained Presbyterian minister and the host of the television show *Mister Rogers' Neighborhood,* had reached out to children across the country with a clear calling to extend love through a calm and creative broadcast. I found myself wondering what he would have thought of my approach to the problem. He was the nation's very definition of the correct treatment of children. Children were drawn to him, Jesus style. It made me wonder, *Was I patient enough when Jaleel's tears started to flow and his tantrum started to escalate into kicking?* I needed a "WWMRD?" bracelet: What Would Mr. Rogers Do? Distract him with puppets or a song? Would his nonthreatening magnetism have melted Jaleel's confused rage? Is the I-like-you-just-the-way-you-are line supposed to work in this situation, in this neighborhood?

Truth was, I really didn't like Jaleel at that moment. I didn't like his mother, who often left him home alone. I didn't like that there was sometimes little food in his fridge. I didn't like the chemical imprint that was left in his body by his mother's addiction, which made him overreact and become violent. I wasn't glad that he was my neighbor, and it wasn't even remotely turning out to be a beautiful day.

No, I don't think Mr. Rogers would have approached the situation as I did. Maybe the problem that needed solving first was *me*—my impatience, my hope of distancing myself from Jaleel's real problems, my judgment of his family situation. The cynics will accuse Mr. Rogers of having offered a white, middle-class love. They'll say his brand of love won't work in the 'hood. And certainly it seems too late for the television reruns of *Mister Rogers' Neighborhood* to have any effect in mine. That world is foreign to Lowell. Jaleel needs everything Mr. Rogers stood for and practiced, but embodied in flesh and blood, a flesh and blood that looks like his. Yet it's clear that I, and the students who experienced this whole episode, needed what Mr. Rogers so obviously had: a deep calling, a single message and a true love of neighbor.

So, what did the action of carrying a screaming child through the neighborhood accomplish in my journey with Jesus? The juxtaposition of Mr. Rogers' neighborhood and Jaleel's is what got the wheels of reflection turning. As we reflected on the situation, the intern who helped me and my partners in ministry revealed my impatience, along with my desire for quick fixes, my concern for my image in the neighborhood and the shallowness of my love. Now, when a child like Jaleel comes along, I know to slow down my responses and involve others in solutions.

The power of this cycle of *action* and *reflection* is widely recognized[1] and is an irreplaceable element in the process of leveraging experience for maximum effectiveness in the growth of the disciple.

JESUS IN ACTION AND REFLECTION

Watching Jesus in action affirms this cycle. In Luke's Gospel, after a pattern of various kinds of *action* in a succession of cities, Jesus paused one evening to have dinner at the home of a religious leader in the city. During this event, a woman, with no thought to the etiquette of the day, crashed the dinner to see Jesus (Lk 7:36-50). She stood by him, weeping, unwittingly letting her tears mix with the dust of his un-washed feet as she crouched in shame. Having nothing to clean up the mud that was created, she used her hair to wipe his feet.

This was undoubtedly an amazing *experience,* both deeply humil-iating and poignant, certainly for the woman and perhaps for every-one. But what the host, Simon, obsessed over was her social class and her sins. He took offense at the presence of this urban "sinner" (v. 37). Jesus used the spontaneous occasion on that night in the city to *reflect* openly about the host's lack of graciousness; Simon had offered no greeting and no foot-washing for his guest (vv. 44-46). Jesus *reflects* on the woman's *actions* in contrast to the host's. In a hospitality-based culture, this failure to provide hospitality was either an intentional slight to Jesus or a gross oversight. Jesus then took the *action* of for-giving her and sent her on her way with a shalom *(eirēnē)* blessing. He then moved out into further urban mission "through cities and villages" (8:1).

The text notes that his disciples were with him (v. 1)—a teaching moment—as were other women struggling with the same issues as the one whom he had reached out to at dinner (v. 2). This notation and the surrounding context underscores how Jesus used spontane-ous experiences in the city to bring spiritual truths to the surface for his followers, particularly truths about a person's character. Jesus' ac-tions affirmed them while calling into question the host's character. His subsequent teaching (vv. 5-8), which recalls the parable of the soils, emphasized a need to keep our hearts soft and fertile toward God's word; Simon's lack of love was evidence of a heart hardened toward the things of God. Jesus then juxtaposed those truths with his mission activities in a potent and recurring cycle of *action* and *reflection*. This cycle was primary in Jesus' cache of training tools for the transformation of those who would follow him.

A child in meltdown and the bizarre spectacle of a woman cleansing Jesus' dirty feet both have the power, through reflection, to lead a person into a process of growth that no amount of good intentions, sheer will or determination can accomplish. Given the amount of stuff we process every day—text messages, conversations, deadlines, requirements, information—most of us are unpracticed in the discipline of reflection. As we engage in compassionate action, the simple act of writing our thoughts, impressions and prayers about the event and the act of telling them to another person become catalytic ingredients for our growth.

5

Fear and Faith

SPIRITUAL SCHOOL OF THE PINK GERANIUM

The Spirit of God orchestrates and designs experiences in our lives. I am convinced these are custom-made, from God's hand. Yet they sometimes come as uninvited and unwelcome guests in our well-ordered existence.

During our thirteen years in Lowell, we have experienced our share of intimidating events. There was so much gunfire in our first few years we developed the ability to distinguish between the shots that needed to be called in and those we knew we could ignore. A young woman involved in the sex industry was shot near our house and came bleeding to our door. We had multiple cars run into in our front yard, cars broken into in our side yard, a car firebombed in our back alley by a neighborhood gang. But, we morbidly joked, these occurrences were at least spread out over a period of years so it was harder to link them together in a chain. We've had moments of panic, but in general we haven't suffered under a chronic climate of fear, which many people assume exists in the heart of a city.

One of those moments of distress happened late one night. The phone rang. It was a neighbor who said that one of the large pots of pink geraniums from our front porch was "walking down the street." My wife, Tina, had cultivated and fertilized and nurtured these plants until they spilled over the top, cascading in a waterfall of pink splendor. These were our pride and joy, a splash of color and a dash of pizzazz for those speeding by on our busy street.

Someone had tried to steal them a year before, only to drop them halfway home. So we had put chunks of cement in the bottom to increase the weight, hoping that would make them harder to carry off. But this night, four guys from the gang house around the corner were apparently having no trouble at all managing the load. Our neighbor had seen where they went and had called the police. That was when the dread started.

I would have let them have the geraniums. After all, they had apparently been drawn to the same thing we had—this incredible display of color. Maybe a little pink in their lives would soften their world. Actually I just didn't think it was wise to confront them. But the police were calling me. Their first question was "What's a geranium?" Then they asked me to come to the gang house and identify a plant they had found in its yard. They would carry it out front.

Were they kidding? Were they new here? You don't do that in this neighborhood! But my sons were urging me to go, my neighbor wanted me to go, the police had asked for me to go. I grudgingly acknowledged that to ignore this was to invite more of it. On the way there, my neighbor whispered to me from the shadows in her front yard, "Don't tell them it was me who called the police."

When I got there, six gang members were sitting on the curb in a row, handcuffed. And there in the middle of the street, in the combined glare of two police cars' headlights, was my pink geranium, its vines trembling in the night air. I felt stupid standing in front of the police and saying, "Yup, that's my geranium alright." But that feeling turned to fear as my son and I lugged it home. I wondered if some of the others in the gang would retaliate.

That night I stayed downstairs to listen. In the dark, with my anxieties swirling around, I remembered a lesser-known prayer of St. Francis.

All Highest, Glorious God
Cast your light into the darkness of my heart.
Give me right faith
Firm hope
Perfect charity
And profound humility
With wisdom of perception, O Lord,
So that I may do what is truly your holy will.

My *actual* experience that night led to the fear of a *potential* experience, and that fear led to reflection and a deepening of my hunger for God. I remember thinking it felt like a spiritual pickax carving out new space in my soul and preparing it for something new that he wanted to plant. This experience chipped away a veneer of confidence about our safety that I had cultivated. It exposed the appearance of grace that I projected toward people who were different, and it laid bare the presence of hatred and repulsion that I had let take root just beneath the surface. It uncovered the reality of who I trusted (for example, the police and our security screen) more than God for our well-being. It revealed that I had regarded these possessions as treasures and that my heart was planted with them. The number and nature of character issues this experience uncovered in me was surprising—at least half a dozen onramps to God's work in my life created in a single night.

The next day we went to get the police report. Reading that report set the lessons that God had in mind deeply into our discipleship, as we gained insight into the lives of the young men. We learned their ages, their family circumstances, how fed up one of the mothers was with her son, how she had given up. These bits of information humanized them in our eyes; it made it easier to begin praying for them and for a chance to meet them. But in a month they were gone from the house altogether.

God had choreographed a life-changing moment that involved a crisis and dilemma, action, reflection and whole-life application. As a result, as apprentices of Jesus, we had new tools and perspectives for similar circumstances: we are a little quicker to pray, a little slower to judge, more sure of God's protection and more aware of the immense needs of the young men who roam these streets.

FROM TENSE TO RIDICULOUS

The theft of our geraniums was a tense but in many ways ridiculous experience that has shaped our discipleship. The dramatic and ridiculous seem to combine well in the city. I hesitate, in fact, to tell you about another experience I had. It is so unsubstantial and embarrassing. But honesty has to be one of the tools in an apprentice's tool belt.

I was trying to sleep in a drafty old building downtown, a former tire factory turned urban mission, which was the site of an urban experiential learning and service project I was running. Outside the massive arched window in the room, the neon lights of the Eazy 8 Motel flashed, and I could hear arguments between men as they passed by. Gunfire echoed occasionally in the background. In the midst of all that noise my sense of dread began to grow. But it was made worse when a large, brown object began to slowly crawl toward the wall opposite my sleeping bag. I watched in the dimness as it traveled over forty feet, finally making it down to my eye level. Trying to ignore it was not an option, as it was the size of my hand. My eyes got bigger and bigger as I strained to see in the darkness.

I finally got up enough courage to flip the light on, even though the creature had moved to a position near the light switch. When I did, I saw the face, yes, the face, of the largest cockroach I had ever encountered, almost four inches long. It was so big I swear it had a facial expression. I grabbed the biggest, flattest object I could find, which happened to be my Bible, and smashed the giant bug up against the wall. The room shook with the force. (God's Word packs a punch.) When I peeled the Bible back, to my dismay the cockroach just sort of shuddered and then merely proceeded to crawl indifferently back up toward the ceiling.

I couldn't sleep the rest of the night. The chaos on the street outside did not bother me as much as that roach did. But that incident gave me insight into my fears and the way I value my safety and comfort above all. I am such a wuss.

It's a good thing we had studied Psalm 55 on that project. King David had to deal with his fears over things that were happening in the city. But this warrior had greater concerns than cockroaches. He was distraught and troubled over the "violence and strife in the city. / Day and night they go around it on its walls, / and iniquity and trouble are within it; / ruin is in its midst; / oppression and fraud / do not depart from its marketplace" (vv. 9-11). David said that he wished he could "fly away and be at rest; / truly, I would flee far away; / I would lodge in the wilderness" (vv. 6-7). Even a king gets scared and wants to get out of the city. But his strategy to deal with his fear was to reflect on God's sovereignty (v. 19) and pray, "But I call upon God, / and the LORD will save me" (v. 16). His strategy was to cast his burden on the Lord, and he believed that he would be sustained (v. 22). He openly and verbally declared his trust in God (v. 23)—another important tool in the belt of the apprentice.

Whether it's a serious threat of retaliation or the ridiculous fears of insects of unusual size, intentional immersion in the context of the city juxtaposed with reflection on the experiences of people in the Bible, who had to figure out what discipleship should look like in their urban context, yields an almost surgical form of transformation in an individual. Part of a radical overhaul, it removes the dead skin of theological ideas that have been acquired without corresponding experience or action. The result of that exfoliation is a fresh sensitivity to the work of God.

6

Involuntary Peel

New skin stings. Sometimes the layers of dead skin are peeled off of us by someone else, before we are ready. That must have been the case for Peter when he visited Paul's work in the amazing city of Antioch. This city was fast becoming the new center of Christendom; in fact, there the followers of Christ were first called Christians (Acts 11:26). Antioch was tremendously multiethnic, a crossroads of culture and trade, and the church reflected that diversity in its leadership (13:1). Cypriot and Cyrenian Christians had planted the church, and Barnabas had fanned it into flame and provided initial leadership. He had retrieved Saul (Paul) from the city of Tarsus, and together they had invested more than a year of their lives in Antioch. Peter, James and John had commissioned Paul and Barnabas to take the gospel to Gentiles and had given them the specific charge to remember the poor, which Paul acknowledged he was especially interested in doing (Gal 2:10). In Antioch, they were faithfully living out their call.

Enter Peter. On an extended visit to observe the growing church in Antioch, though his own calling was primarily to preach the gospel to Jewish people, he clearly got into the spirit of crosscultural evangelism. Perhaps he was remembering his experience with Cornelius and the lessons God taught him about showing no partiality. He had undergone personal transformation on this issue to the extent that he had passionately presented the case for the Gentiles in front of the other Jewish leaders in Jerusalem (Acts 15:6-11). The result was that they had drawn up a document validating the work in Antioch and had sent other leaders with Paul and Barnabas to minister there. Now Peter was visiting that work and, it seems, enjoying it as he routinely ate with the new Gentile believers.

But as soon as certain Jewish representatives of the Jerusalem church also came to visit, Peter stopped eating with his new Gentile friends (Gal 2:12). The Bible says that he was afraid of those leaders, perhaps of what they would think of him, perhaps of the negative fallout of identifying with non-Jewish believers. Perhaps he feared that his reputation and standing in the majority-culture church back home would be tarnished. Suddenly all of those lessons he had learned through rooftop visions and through his experience at Cornelius's house, all of the risks he had taken in presenting the case for the Gentiles to the mother church in Jerusalem, all of the leadership he had exercised in arranging for the validation of the new church in Antioch got *compartmentalized*. Those lessons were valid and the transformation in his thinking was real and had led to specific, fruitful outcomes, but the moment those visitors came, he chose to push his new perspective aside. Fear will do that to you.

When Paul saw Peter pulling away from non-Jewish believers, he knew what had to happen. How was this supposed to make the relatively new Gentile believers feel? The church had said that they were full members, but Peter's behavior could send no other message than "You are second-class citizens." Other leaders in the church had begun to imitate Peter's hypocrisy. It had to be dealt with immediately. Paul confronted Peter in public, in front of all the believers (Gal 2:11-14).

The fresh skin of Peter's new perspective from his experience with Cornelius was being tested.

Now use your imagination. If you are Peter, how are you feeling right now? You are an acknowledged pillar of the church (Gal 2:9), a person of great importance from Jerusalem, the starting place of the Christian faith. You actually worked alongside Jesus for three years and of you Jesus himself said, "You are Peter, and on this rock I will build my church" (Mt 16:18). And now your hypocrisy is being publicly exposed. Ministry in this fast-growing, unfamiliar urban church has instantly uncovered the cracks in your theology, the weak spots in your spiritual infrastructure. And all this came about from a decision as simple as who to eat with.

UPSIDE-DOWN CAKE

Food will do that to you. During a summer-long urban internship, Kathy, a Chinese American, was assigned to live with Tamika and Naomi, two African Americans, in a tiny apartment in the Dorchester community of Boston. They were to spend a summer serving in the neighborhood and learning about issues key to ministry in the city, especially what the Bible says about racial reconciliation. All of them were excited about this, because they each felt committed to this value. But none of them guessed how early that value would be tested.

For their first dinner, Kathy took the entire afternoon to prepare a traditional Chinese meal. When Tamika and Naomi were seated at the table she presented her meal, and they said a prayer of thanks. Then Tamika and Naomi reached for some hot sauce that they had brought with them and poured it over the meal. Kathy was horrified and deeply insulted.

It took a while before Kathy felt free to disclose how it had made her feel. At first Tamika and Naomi couldn't understand why it was such a big deal. They just liked hot sauce and felt it enhanced everything it was put on. But eventually Kathy was able to share that, in Chinese tradition, when a meal is presented, it is complete. To alter it means that it was defective. And to reject a person's food is to unwittingly reject her culture and identity. This was a hard conversation, and they all felt the sting of new skin exposed. But in the end they achieved mutual understanding.

Three weeks later that understanding was put to the test. It was Kathy's turn to cook again, and she chose to prepare another traditional Chinese meal. Everybody was feeling pretty comfortable with each other and had forgotten the incident on their first night. After the prayer, Tamika and Naomi instinctively began to reach for the bottles of hot sauce but caught themselves halfway, their hands frozen in midair. They started to apologize and Kathy laughed. "No, it's okay, go ahead," she said with a smile. All three women had begun to think differently in the midst of their crosscultural encounter.

THINKING DIFFERENTLY

Christian discipleship has some characteristics that are common in developmental theory. A person's development, much like discipleship, is more than mere growth or change. Behaviorist Laurent Daloz has shown that "development seems to happen not in a gradual and linear way but in distinct and recognizable leaps."[1] These leaps are often sparked by the juxtaposition of dramatic experience with reflection, followed by action and application, all key elements in experiential discipleship.

How do we know actual development is taking place in our relationship with God? Much of Western Christianity has taught us to measure that based on our increased knowledge of the Bible or increased practice of disciplines such as prayer, worship and fasting. But, as Daloz says, development is more than the acquisition of information. This is obvious as we watch children develop. "A ten-year-old does not simply know more than a four-year-old; she *thinks* differently,"[2] he points out. By the end of the summer internship, Kathy, Tamika and Naomi were thinking differently. After his public confrontation and rebuke by Paul, Peter certainly thought differently, evidenced by the fact that he continued to show concern for the Gentiles (1 Pet 2:12) and to have respect for Paul, whom he subsequently called his beloved brother and whom he acknowledged wrote with wisdom (2 Pet 3:15). The fresh skin from his encounter with Cornelius had been tested and toughened by Paul's sharp reminder that God shows no favoritism.

When we think of discipleship—that is, the process of growth associated with being an apprentice to Christ—we understand that a series of shifts must take place. Daloz contends that there is a range of ways by which we "make meaning" in our lives,[3] that is, by which we find significance or purpose. As we mature we use different criteria to measure how meaningful things are to us. For example, someone who has not yet been amazed by the way Jesus values people in the Gospels may not be making that a priority in his or her own relationships. Those who have been tutored by Jesus find great meaning and satisfaction in treating people as Jesus did. Or take those who have not yet been exposed to the language of justice in the Scriptures. They may not yet feel compelled to build a commitment to justice into their lifestyle decisions. But those who have been captured by Jesus' modeling of justice regard it as a central indicator of the health of their relationship with God. These shifts, often called "perspective transformation,"[4] mean we have begun thinking in whole new ways.

Turning Away and Turning Toward

This new thinking is transformation in the biblical sense of the term.

The biblical writers used the Greek word *metanoia* to convey the essence of what it means to turn away from something. *Metanoia* means repentance, a change of mind leading to a change of direction. A similar concept is found in the word *metamorphosis,* that miraculous process represented best by the change that transforms a caterpillar into a butterfly.

Inherently all true and deep change involves both a turning *away* from something and a turning *toward* something else. It involves a rejection and an embrace. We are learning how to reject—to turn away from hypocrisy (the man at my door), unacknowledged wealth (Kundara), impatience (Jaleel), low expectations of inner-city kids (Napoleon), irrational fears (a giant cockroach), lack of faith (pink geraniums) and other faults too numerous to mention.

But this metamorphosis has meant more than repentance. It has also meant turning *toward* something, an embrace of something. Our neighborhood is teaching my family and me to embrace people who are different and to expect wisdom from them that looks less like knowledge or information and more like experience. As we have become involved in various coalitions seeking to repair and renew the neighborhood, life in Lowell has helped us embrace a more people-centered existence and recapture a sense of responsibility to the whole community, rather than to only our family. Life in the context of poverty has given us a more missional posture and has increased our commitment to helping the church be outward in its orientation.

As I look back on more than a decade here, I can see a heightened presence of many of the Beatitudes in our lives (Mt 5:3-12). For example, we have grown *poor in spirit* as we have experienced powerlessness in the face of urban forces. Sometimes we just don't know what to do. We are not in control and have no good response. We are empty-handed.

We've grown in a *hunger and thirst for righteousness* and justice as we have observed the despair generated by destructive forces eating away at the dignity of the addicted and the oppressed. This afternoon Tina spent time with a woman in the neighborhood who is being taken advantage of by addicted family members, acquaintances and her landlord; she needs to find new housing for herself and her two small children. We are working hard and long for a just solution to her problems, struggling through the complex mixture of her own poor choices and the ways she is being taken advantage of.

We've grown in *mercy* and *peacemaking* as we have been caught between children, parents, gangs and opposing interests so prevalent in the neighborhood. Because our experiences put us in the middle of interpersonal and neighborhood conflicts, we understand and can see better what the gospel contributes to resolution.

These embraces—these things we are turning toward—irritate our new skin, which is uncallused, tender and sensitive But they are unmistakable in their presence as evidences of our growth in Christ.

7

The Smell of Shalom

KARLY AND CASSIE

Some things can't be explained to people. For certain lessons, you need to be able to point to something. If our role is to be disciples, to turn to and embrace the things of Christ, how will we know when it's happening in our lives? By some cognitive measurement? By some theological quiz? Again, in a marvelous gift from God, the city has given me something to point to: the experience of shalom.

Shalom isn't easy to get your arms around as a concept, and its expansiveness makes it hard to explain. It has no single English word as an equivalent. In the Bible, *shalom* means justice, it means peace, it means plenty and abundance, it means security. According to author Perry Yoder, it means a combination of righteousness and justice, making things the way they should be *in* people, *between* people and *for* people.[1] According to Nicholas Wolterstorff, "Shalom is the human being dwelling at peace in all his or her relationships: with God, with self, with fellows, with nature."[2]

On a clear winter day in a neighbor's yard, the city handed me a shalom moment, not as a concept or theological construct, but as an experience. It happened as I watched an onramp being constructed for a neighborhood child before my very eyes, a connection to God's shalom kingdom.

I was standing in the side of the yard of Marty and Joanie Martin, where we held a tutoring program for neighborhood children, watching the kids play soccer before the program began. Marty and Joanie had created a parklike place for them. Florescent, backlit leaves were dancing in a welcoming rhythm above my head. The only girl on the field was dribbling the ball around all the boys and scoring the only goals, her navy-blue school jumper and her long, black hair flying behind her. Most of the boys were Mexican and anxious to prove their abilities at this, their national sport. But they could only grunt in desperation as she passed them all. After the game ended I tried to introduce myself to her.

"Hi, what's your name?" I asked. She studied my mouth as I spoke, looking at me with a blank stare, her hair framing her face like a refugee's scarf. She didn't answer.

"Hola, cómo te llamas?" I said, happy to use one of the few phrases of Spanish I knew. Again, there was no answer, only the careful attention of her passive eyes, which searched my own.

Cassie, who has serious eyes and a responsible air about her for a third-grader, came by and nonchalantly said, "Her name is Karly. She's my cousin and she doesn't speak Spanish," but she gave no clue to Karly's silence.

We called the kids to come into the tutoring center, the "reading club," as we call it. It is filled with books, computers, art materials, games and play equipment. We have crammed thirty kids and tutors into this twelve-by-thirteen space at times. That day I was thankful that we had neither the heat of summer nor the sticky humidity of rain. It was a beautiful day; the kids brought the smell of the field in with them.

Karly brushed her dark, sweaty locks away from her face, revealing a misshapen ear—and a hearing aid. Cassie stayed close to her cousin, choosing some books and a game. Karly mostly observed, not speaking much. She kept to the edges, to the small table and to her cousin. She didn't speak to the boys she had just beaten at their sport. But she observed them at the computer, and she looked with longing at the game they were playing on it. I could see the wheels turning; she wanted to beat them at that too.

When the day ended, I waved goodbye to Karly and Cassie, and they both waved back. Cassie ran across the street to her house, where her father was angry about something, and yelling. She ended up in tears. The brightness of the day was offset by a darkness in her soul.

For weeks it was the same story, my words of welcome notwithstanding. Karly did not speak to me, but she came, she watched, she stayed close to Cassie, she lined up for the treat at the end, she left to go home. I found myself wondering what I could do to engage her.

It was a dark and rainy Thursday, the day for reading club. The sharp brilliance of early winter light was replaced by a cozy drippiness, a wet shroud of permission to stay inside. There were fewer children and no soccer game. We gathered the kids in the room, turned the heat on, said a prayer of thanks for the rain and let them choose their activity. I sat in the black Naugahyde computer chair and Cassie came to me with a book. As I began to read it aloud, she stood behind my left shoulder, following closely. My heart jumped as Karly left her spot by the door, came to stand at my left arm and put her ear close to my mouth. She instantly became engrossed in the story. *This is new,* I thought to myself. *They are focused, interested, at ease.*

A few minutes later I was vaguely aware that there was movement on my shoulder. Cassie was absently trailing her fingers along the seam of my blue denim shirt, tracing the outline of the shoulder piece. I kept reading, and I noticed her focus had not diminished. Both girls were laughing at the story. Then there was more movement, this time at my left side. As I read, Karly began playing with the hair on my left arm. She would gather it up and stand it at a point then comb it down into rows. I stole glances from the corner of my eye as I read. She was into the story; she was not into the hair. She was acting in unself-conscious innocence and trust. For a holy moment, my soul was immersed in a peaceful bath of thankfulness that I was alive for such an apparently mundane but significant event.

I remember thinking, *Why is this affecting me the way it is? Why am I happy, with tears welling up in my eyes? Their situation has not changed.* They were still poor, like all the others. Karly still struggled to connect with the other children, who had no trouble hearing. Cassie still went home to a father whose anger overflowed in shouting. They would grow to be young women and have to deal with the pressures and influences of the neighborhood. Many just like them are pregnant by the time they're fifteen. Over and over I had seen it happen. Nothing of importance had changed.

But in that moment, they tasted the beauty and light of an hour with no shadows. They were safe and at peace. No doubt, I infused it with far more significance than it probably deserved. I should have cared more about the systems and structures that were shaping their lives. But in that holy moment I did not. If nothing was changed, something was added. There was a place to go, someone nonthreatening with hairy arms to sit with, a room without shadows and a space in the world where laughter is real and dreams seem possible. There is a shalom pathway to a new life. This is what I have turned to, what I have embraced.

It has been seven years since the encounter. Karly is in high school now, and the city newspaper has just published a letter she wrote to the editor on a subject that she is passionate about: how people who are different are treated. She's going to be okay. My embrace of shalom is partly due to that experience with her and Cassie and the reflection and observation it sparked. At that time it became clear to me what we were aiming at in the neighborhood and how God would build his peace into my life as a byproduct.

Epilogue to Part 1

The Bible describes Jesus as one able to "sympathize with our weaknesses" (Heb 4:15), who "lived among us" (Jn 1:14)—"moved into the neighborhood," as Eugene Peterson translates it in *The Message*. Jesus "emptied himself, / taking the form of a slave, / being born in human likeness. / . . . And . . . humbled himself" (Phil 2:7-8). The heart of God could be fully revealed only by the incarnation, the act and experience of becoming human, of placing himself in the very context of suffering that he wanted to redeem. Perhaps this same formula is true for human beings. Perhaps who we are can't be seen or known fully until we are placed in circumstances we do not control.

God has used repeated cycles of experience, reflection, whole-life application and action to catalyze the transformational process in my family and me. God also has used experiences to accomplish makeovers in countless others who have sought to incarnate the gospel of shalom in inner-city neighborhoods. It is turning us into what some have called "reflective practitioners," those whose knowledge, experience and reflective posture actively engage with our context.[1]

Yet experiential discipleship in the city can accomplish more than just a personal internal makeover. It has the power to uncover the very real but often hidden forces that are shaping everyday life there. Exposing and understanding those forces is the basis for real transformation at a community level. Perhaps that's what's behind the promise of God that our own well-being is wrapped up in seeking the well-being of the city: "But seek the welfare [shalom] of the city where I have sent you into exile, and pray to the LORD on its behalf, for in its welfare [shalom] you will find your welfare [shalom]" (Jer 29:7).

Each of the chapters in part two shows how experience in the city acts as an onramp to God's highway to the shalom kingdom. Experiential discipleship does this by uncovering specific forces that are silently and invisibly distorting the lives of many vulnerable people, special objects of interest for the shalom King. I won't try to be comprehensive by highlighting all of the forces in the city. I will explore just a few of the ones I have experienced or observed, reflected on, and tried to make a modest difference in.

PART 2

Accelerate

GETTING UP TO SPEED

ON THE CITY

8

Hidden Forces

**PAY NO ATTENTION TO
THE MAN BEHIND THE CURTAIN**

It's a no-brainer: Crime loves the dark. Apparently, so does bureaucracy. When the streetlights in our neighborhood went out during our first year there, we were nervous. After a few days we began to call the city to see what the problem was. In our neighborhood, this event was more than a mere inconvenience; it was a security issue. The city staff said they were "working on it." (That's city-speak for "What? There's a problem?") Three months later they were "still working on it."

Finally the city admitted that the problem was caused by someone they romantically referred to as "the copper-wire bandit." Apparently a homeless man had discovered that if he removed the faceplate off the base of the old pineapple lampposts that lined the street, he could pull up the copper ground wire for about a hundred yards. He would ball it up and take it to recyclers, where it would fetch a good price. Then he would move up the street and pull up the next section. Apparently he had done this for several miles. The official position was, "We don't want to fix the problem until we've caught the man." (That's city-speak for "We secretly admire the guy and have placed bets on how many miles he will go up the same road.")

A few of us who had intentionally relocated to the neighborhood to seek its shalom met regularly to pray and act on its behalf. We agreed that if this had taken place in the wealthy part of town, the lights would have stayed off for no more than three days before a solution had been found. Now, more than three months later, the city was in no hurry. We figured that they must not have received many complaints from the neighborhood, making them believe they could take their time. So some of us started calling City Hall regularly. But other neighbors, many of whom do not have proper documentation, were afraid to join us. They would suffer in the dark rather than risk attention from the authorities.

Even those who are not afraid to complain still often find it difficult to navigate the complexities of civic bureaucracies. They are passed around from department to department, feel they are not listened to and stop trying altogether. Then new residents move in and assume it's normal for the lights not to work. Those in the middle class, however, know not only which department to contact at City Hall but also the tone of voice to use when it appears that no action is being taken. It is second nature to us. It is our assumption that streetlights should work and that, when they don't, the city should fix them immediately. It's what we pay our taxes for.

A full four months later, after many calls, the lights came back on, even though the city still had not caught "the copper-wire bandit." Back when I was living in the suburbs, if I had heard about the lights being out in Lowell, I would have assumed that the city was doing its best and that there must be a good reason for the delay. But after living there, being affected by the problem, listening to my neighbors, trying to get the city to listen to the needs of my neighbors, I realized invisible forces were operating. These forces included the city's assumption that the poor and uneducated residents of Lowell would not put pressure on the city to act; the city's habit of diverting funds that had been earmarked for Lowell to other projects elsewhere, knowing that few residents of the neighborhood would notice; and the realities of social class and race that shape the relationship people have with the authorities. Digging deeper, I realized they also included the politics and competing interests of a street that connected the districts of two city council people. These forces and doubtless others combined to delay repairs.

GOSPEL SUBJECTS?

We had to wrestle with the question of whether streetlights are a gospel issue in the same way that prayer or evangelism is. Certainly we could see the obvious: God would want people to be safe and light serves an important purpose in a neighborhood that suffers high levels of crime. But could we see that we had an obligation to pursue equal access to city services—in other words, justice for people who had no voice? And what about being confrontational in the face of inaction? Was that okay? Could we peel back the layers of excuses to the real reasons the lights were not being fixed? Was this a gospel activity?

When we discovered that the streets had not been repaved in the neighborhood for forty years because the money earmarked for that purpose had been diverted elsewhere, would the gospel compel us to address that? When we found that the city was not enforcing codes in our neighborhood, allowing absentee landlords to neglect their properties and ignore the complaints of the tenants about mold or malfunctioning heating systems or unusable toilets or dangerous electrical systems, would the gospel have anything to say? Lampposts? Asphalt? Toilets? Are these gospel issues?

To see them as such requires a bit of unmasking. Those problems are the outcome of forces and powers aligned against the shalom that

God has intended for human communities. As the apostle Paul wrote, "Our struggle is not against enemies of blood and flesh, but against the rulers, against the authorities, against the cosmic powers of this present darkness" (Eph 6:12). Some in the church imagine demons floating above cities, in charge of wreaking havoc. As evidence that angels and demons are assigned to individual cities, they cite the angel in the book of Daniel, who said he was delayed aiding Daniel because he was at war with the prince of Persia (Dan 10:13). Perhaps that is valid evidence. But when simple, run-of-the-mill human sin, corruption, favoritism or sheer laziness enters the systems of a city, the effect is the same. Filipina theologian and activist Melba Maggay rightly calls these the "depersonalized forces of evil at work in the social climate . . . or entrenched in structures of the created order."[1]

Instead of being territorial demons, perhaps the powers and principalities are closer to what theologian and community organizer Robert Linthicum describes when exploring the relationship between the economic, political and religious systems of a city. According to his understanding of the vision of Deuteronomy, the worship of God should lead to a political system that establishes justice. A just political system ensures the growth of economic systems that promote stewardship of the commonwealth. But when these systems become infected by human sin, they act as a networked web of injustice. Instead of the worship of God informing how political and economic systems should operate, economic systems become the primary engine running a city. The financial bottom line becomes the most important quest, influencing a city's political process. Religious leaders are co-opted into this system, their roles degenerating into the performance of insignificant religious functions, such as public prayers that validate civic ceremonies, as their dependence on the system grows.[2]

When Jesus confronted the Pharisees for neglecting justice (Mt 23:23), he was confronting an interdependent network in which religious leaders had become the beneficiaries of a system of advantage, ironically propped up by a corrupt, occupying Roman force. Alfonso Weiland, director of the Peruvian human rights organization Peace and Hope, writes, "We need to unmask the social systems in order to transform them."[3]

Author and activist Graham Gordon notes that the psalms often refer to God's judgment on political authorities who do not pursue justice. Officials are called to "defend the cause of the weak and fatherless; / maintain the rights of the poor and oppressed. / Rescue the weak and needy; / deliver them from the hand of the wicked" (Ps 82:3-4 NIV). Gordon writes, "The weaker members of society are often powerless to withstand abuses of economic or political power by other groups and the role of the state is to ensure justice is done and that the poor do not simply become victims of the survival of the fittest."[4]

What led to my reflection about power as a force shaping life in the city and eventually to my participation in some holy pestering of the powers? Three things: (1) being in the dark, (2) being in a position to act with others who were in the dark, and (3) the light of the gospel, which assumes we will act on behalf of the vulnerable. It was the juxtaposition of complete darkness in a crime-ridden neighborhood with opportunities to reflect on God's concern for justice among the privileged and the powerless. The experience of that juxtaposition functioned like Toto, Dorothy's dog in *The Wizard of Oz*, dragging back the curtain to reveal the wizard, a mundane little man pulling levers and pushing buttons. Experience has the power to uncloak what is hidden.

9

Paul's Urban Tour

THE FORCE OF IDENTITY

Maybe Dorothy's "We're not in Kansas anymore" echoes what people unaccustomed to the city feel as they walk its streets for the first time. Many of them wonder how the gospel will ever permeate and redeem the city, ever connect with the complex blend of culture and language, ever even be noticed in the midst of an endless parade of choices and options.

Even experienced urban missionaries and inner-city practitioners can become distressed and overwhelmed in a city because its sheer size and complexity make it appear unreachable. The apostle Paul was an experienced urban practitioner who specifically chose the cities of the Greek and Roman world as strategic "megaphones"[1] to amplify the transforming message of the gospel to the diverse people who cross-pollinated from city to city. Acts 16 describes Paul's ambitious and extensive tour of cities, which included Derbe, Lystra, Troas, Neapolis, Philippi, Thessalonica, Berea and Athens, one after another.

Acts 17 tells us that upon arriving in Athens Paul engaged in a classic experiential discipleship method. Today we would call it a "windshield survey": touring a city to collect as much data as possible. Paul was interested in what drove the place. He himself alluded to some of the features of the reconnaissance, and the narrator filled in the gaps. Through that process we get a sense of what it took to understand some of the forces shaping life there. We learn that Paul made several connections almost immediately, crossing diverse sectors as he went. He interacted with the *religious* community of the city as he presented his case in the synagogue. He placed himself in the *marketplace,* using random encounters with those who were there to present his message. He also interacted with the *academy* as he presented his philosophy to the academicians, the Stoics and Epicureans, educated intellectuals whose interest he was successful at stirring.

NONACCIDENTAL TOURIST

Like all good communicators he was gathering intelligence while he was interacting. We learn something of his straightforward methodology for uncovering hidden forces in the city when, in speaking at the Areopagus, he referred to his first experience in Athens. He remarked mundanely, "For as I *went through* the city and *looked carefully* . . ." (Acts 17:23, italics mine). Paul got out in the city and looked, paying attention to things he saw. He knew that they had meaning and would give him clues that would help him connect with the city in a way that might bring a measure of transformation. Interestingly, the text takes note of the impact of Paul's observations on his *own* life. It says that he was "deeply distressed" by what he saw (v. 16). Another translation says his spirit was "provoked."

We might ask why Paul was distressed. He had been in other religiously pluralistic cultures. He had just finished a massive tour of pagan cities. Rampant idolatry was not new to him. Perhaps it was the sheer concentration of Athens, the confused religious thinking, the number of options for belief that affected him so. He *experienced* the city; this was no mere detached exercise. We can see the passion behind his message and the sense of urgency as he sought to invite the Athenians into the kingdom of God. As part of that message, Paul quoted one of their own poets. How did he know to do that? And when did he have time to read the poetry of this culture and even to commit some of it to memory? Was there a used bookstore in the agora?

IDENTITY, IDENTITY, IDENTITY

As we watch Paul's experiential strategy in Athens, we see a practitioner intentionally connecting with what might be called a *trinity of identity markers* in a city. Cities, much like people, have characteristics, even identities, that influence its residents. Father Ben Beltran, the pastor of a large scavenger community living on the vast garbage dump called Smoky Mountain in Manila, has helped me understand that specific clues to every city's identity can be understood through discernment of the *urbs,* the *civitas* and the *anima.*

The *urbs* (from which we get our word *urban*) comprise the infrastructure of the city, including the physical layout, transportation systems, garbage collection, sewage, human interaction with the environment and so on. A lot can be learned about a city by observing these mundane realities. How do they affect the lives of those who live there? Do they affect everyone equally? Paul's windshield survey got him out into the city, giving him a view of the lay of the land. For instance, he could see by the placement of statues which gods stood watch over the academy, over the marketplace and over the synagogue.

The *urbs*—the way a city is set up—influence the degree to which citizens benefit from a city's systems. For example, many in my neighborhood do not have a car. Yet the evening bus service downtown was not available after six o'clock for years after it was terminated due to the downtown's decline. Other parts of the city had bus service until midnight. Or consider the fact that the entire west side of Fresno had not one major grocery store or bank, so the residents had to rely on more expensive mom-and-pop shops and check-cashing institutions. Garbage collection was not handled well in my neighborhood; the trash often spilled from the trucks, and the people had no recourse. Worse yet, people from outside the neighborhood would come at night and dump used tires and broken televisions. The city did not diligently enforce codes, diminishing safety and encouraging further decay. The forces of the *urbs* weigh on people's daily lives in my neighborhood, while for many others in the city, the *urbs* seem set up for them, automatically making their lives easier.

The *civitas* (from which we get our word *civic*) of a city has to do with its behaviors, its attitudes, its characteristics and its networks of people. These are often unique and discernible. For example, if I were to ask you what Paris is known for, you may think of couples kissing beneath the Eiffel Tower or cuddling in cafés in the Latin Quarter, and say, "Romance." If I asked what Wall Street is known for, you might say money or power. For Hollywood, you might say glamour or excess.

If I had to summarize Fresno's *civitas,* I would say it is uneven toil, uneven benefit under the hot sun. Though the area's multibillion-dollar agricultural output feeds and clothes the world, sending fruits of every kind, nuts and world-class crops of cotton to all parts of the globe, nearly four out of ten children live under the poverty line, only 16 percent of adults have been to college, and only 33 percent have graduated from high school. Unemployment runs between 11 and 16 percent. The classes do not mix; there are clear boundaries that the affluent do not voluntarily cross.

How do we get a feel for the *civitas* of a city? Paul's networking among diverse sectors of Athens, ranging from customers and tradespeople in the marketplace to philosophers and academicians in the halls of learning, gave him a feel for how to craft a message that made sense to a few of them. The few who did respond (including Dionysius and Damaris)[2] had the ability to access spheres of influence that could have led to extensive transformation in the city. The *civitas* of a city acts as a force shaping relationships between the sectors, ways of doing business, questions of who has access to power and policy-making, and the workings of public and private institutions that shape people's experience of life there.

The *anima* of a city can be tricky to understand. It has to do with what Father Ben Beltran calls the "unconscious universe" of the residents, the unspoken assumptions about God or about what governs and guides the people's existence. It often includes religious distinctives. Perhaps it is akin to what we might call the "soul" of the city.

In my city this might include the particular brand of folk Catholicism practiced by many of the Mexican immigrants who make up a majority here. It might include a legacy of invisible power and influence practiced by large land developers who, for years, dictated the way the city was run. It might include a horrible self-image that Fresno defaulted to when at one time it was proclaimed by an annual national report to be the least livable city in the United States. It recently also has been branded as having the highest rate of concentrated poverty in the nation.[3] All of these give clues to the *anima*, the soul of our city. When Paul quoted one of the Athenians' own poets, he was seeking to touch the *anima* of the city, using the language of the heart. One gets a feel for *anima* by listening to what people in all sectors of the city talk about, what they assume, what they depend on.

Paul's urban tour formed his strategy for unveiling the forces that shaped the perspectives, behaviors and beliefs of Athens. Once revealed, he would plant seeds that would take root in uniquely Athenian soil, an urban garden like no other. By A.D. 139 the Christian community in Athens was large enough for Hygeinos, the bishop of Rome, to notice what was happening and write them a letter. Subsequent leaders of the church in Athens imitated Paul's effective apologetic style. In the second century, Bishop Quadratus addressed Emperor Hadrian, and Aristides addressed Emperor Marcus Aurelius, both from Athenian soil.[4] By the sixth century, many of the major pagan temples, including the Parthenon on the Areopagus, had been converted into Christian churches. Churches sprouted up on the very hill Paul had preached on and in the marketplace as well, just part of the legacy of his investment in understanding the identity of Athens.

When followed by reflection and action, experience in the city can reveal the essence of its identity. But that still leaves the following question: Once the essence of a city is revealed—its *urbs*, its *civitas* and its *anima*—could the church address those things that define it and serve it as Jesus would have?

10

Zorro and the California Pepper

To be sure, Paul's strategy in Athens and the surrounding Greek cities took some forethought and intentionality. Because the apostle found himself in new urban settings, investigation was crucial. But when you live in the heart of a city, the rhythms and realities of that place, which might be invisible to people on the outside, can present themselves to you point-blank. No investigation needed.

That's what happened one beautiful afternoon in Lowell. My family and I had put on our best clothes and were headed for the front yard to take a family picture. We never made it off the porch but instead stood there frozen, watching a man shuffle slowly up to our large, shady tree. He had on a black cape that flowed behind him and black leather boots that looked two sizes too big for him; they were slipping off his heels. He wore a wide-brimmed black hat and a red sash around his neck. That's right, it was Zorro standing in our yard, and he was talking to our tree.

Actually, he was arguing with it. I couldn't imagine that it was the tree's fault. It's a very modest and lowly California pepper tree, with a twisted and knotted trunk and wisps of lacy, green, fernlike branches swaying innocently in the breeze. It's incapable of sarcasm or insult. But he scolded it for several minutes before turning to leave. Then, in an afterthought, he changed his mind. He stopped and raised his voice at our tree in what could only have been an ancient curse in a blend of Spanish and Mixtec Indian, with a few curses in English as well, apparently thrown in for good measure. We watched as he shuffled off.

In subsequent days we got to know this Zorro a bit. His name was Raymond; he lived in a group home down the street. We learned he got his boots from a dumpster, presumably the same place his black felt hat and cape had come from. I imagined brown leaves of discarded lettuce still hanging from the edge as it emerged, a treasure in his hands. He was only in his forties, but could have used a senior citizen card, no problem. Years of drinking and living in alleys had taken their toll on his appearance and his mind. Having a conversation with him was difficult, as there were only small intervals when he was lucid. Most of the time his words were convoluted, as twisted as the limbs of our California pepper tree.

When Zorro appears in your front yard and talks to your tree, it gets your attention. Suddenly we began to notice and take an interest in all the other people wandering about the neighborhood having conversations with themselves, some at the top of their lungs. Grady looks like he just finished shooting a scene from *Night of the Living Dead* or maybe *Tales from the Crypt*. Thin as a needle, he carries a coat with him everywhere, even if it's a hundred degrees. Greg always looks like someone just told him a dirty joke, and he repeats things over and over to himself. Betty, a petite, white-haired woman, eats out of dumpsters and acts skittish, as if people are following her.

We also became aware of the disproportionate number of board-and-care homes and halfway houses on our street. We learned that many of them were not registered or licensed, and unscrupulous managers or owners often exploited their vulnerable tenants. We learned about the direct impact of budget cuts in social services on the lives of these neighbors. We learned about the strong connection between mental illness and homelessness or transience.

ZORRO IN GERASENE

Not long after Raymond appeared under our tree, we rediscovered the story of Jesus encountering a man living among the tombs in Gentile territory (Mk 5:1-20). He was *crazy*. People tried to restrain him with chains, but he broke them. He ran around naked, howling at the moon. Turns out, multiple voices were speaking to him; demons were tormenting him to the point of insanity. Jesus figured this out right away and healed him. He sent the demons into a herd of pigs that, in a spectacular dramatization of the destructive intent of the demons, rushed headlong into the water to their deaths. People were surprised to see the man clothed again and sitting calmly in his right mind. He asked Jesus if he could join his company and follow him, but in typical fashion, Jesus was more concerned about restoring this man to his community than he was about getting a celebrity convert. He sent him home to his family.

Raymond, Betty, Grady and Greg all live in the confusion of multiple voices, and they are dying a slow death. So far, there has been no herd of pigs to dramatize the destructive end of those voices. And most cities have few strategies and limited means to deal with deranged and disturbed souls who wander in the care and custody of the streets, or each other. Worse yet, in my city of 450 churches, there is no coordinated attempt to deal with the vast issue of mental illness among the poor of Fresno. It isn't even discussed.

Yet the untreated mentally ill create a very solitary burden to overwhelmed extended family members, many of whom are suffering silently in the church. The homeless mentally ill clog city services and clinics, and scare the general populace away from the districts of town where they wander, creating a ripple effect of economic distress and collapse. Could the church address this vast need? What would we need to do to get organized, to be equipped? What things might we do to empower the many health-care professionals sitting in the pew? How could we minister to family members of the mentally ill? Could 450 churches collaborate to provide specialized training that would travel from church to church? Could we fund a residential center?

These questions came to me only because I overheard Raymond's conversation with my tree, a tree planted by a sidewalk where the homeless mentally ill pace back and forth, to and from nowhere—a place where God's people could be, at the very least to provide conversation with a real human rather than with bark.

11

An Undetected Wave

THE FORCE OF HUMANITY IN MOTION

We think the ground underneath us is solid, but it is shifting all the time. Plates, faults and underground aquifers hide very real forces—forces concealed until there is a tsunami, a sinkhole or an earthquake. Then we are reminded of the power of the unseen.

Many forces in the city are like that. Minor, gradual changes are not noticed until a critical mass is reached. In Hong Kong, the revised form of capitalism that functions under China's watchful eye allows for the stratification of wealth, resulting in vast disparities between rich and poor. This city of skyscrapers struggles on the one hand to provide enough employment, but on the other hand must import international labor, primarily Filipino women, to serve as domestic workers for people of means. These women are not allowed to bring their men, because entry-level jobs for male laborers are scarce and are reserved for Hong Kong men. The number of these women has grown slowly to more than 150,000 in that city alone. They are paid very little, have only one day off per week, are often exploited and have no protection, no voice in the society and no political representation. This is but one example of a worldwide trend in economic migration, a massive movement of the earth under our feet. Worldwide, the predominant type of migrant is a young, unmarried woman.[1]

Today more than 150 million people live in a country they were not born in. About 13 million of those are refugees; the rest voluntarily left their homeland to seek a better life.[2] You wouldn't know about the presence of the female domestic workers in Hong Kong unless you happened to be in Statue Park, in the heart of the city, on a Sunday afternoon. There, fourteen thousand young women gather every week to support one another, to get news from home and to try to navigate together the complexities of life in the migrant stream. As I walked in this massive gathering on a recent study trip, the presence of human sharks swimming around these women became obvious. The women are vulnerable prey for con men in the very place they have gathered for safety and support.

A church in the heart of the Kowloon district of the city has only recently noticed this trend, though it has been developing for a decade, and they have begun praying about an appropriate form of outreach and response. Some have helped to organize demonstrations on behalf of the women.

In São Paulo, Brazil—where more than half the population are immigrants—the church is experiencing explosive growth, largely due to its readiness to reach out in practical love to these people when they most need it, offering economic help, child care and friendship. But so many churches are still designing outreach that makes sense in monoethnic contexts, without regard for the realities and changing rules of life in a migrant stream.

A FORCE FOR CHANGE

The same force is influencing my own city and state. More than half of California's residents were not born there. The population of the Fresno valley has doubled in the past thirty years and is projected to double again in the next thirty, with a growth rate higher than anywhere in the United States and, more significantly, faster than many less-developed countries, including Mexico. Most of this growth is due to migration. Interestingly, as migrants (many of whom have low levels of educational attainment) swell the Fresno population, the majority of those leaving are white, and 24 percent of those have college degrees.[3]

These forces touch literally every aspect of life. New urban dwellers coming from developing countries arrive with little experience working in a legal economy and often reproduce economic patterns developed in an underground economy, such as black-market sales and noncompliance with codes, permits and licensing.[4] Immigrants are often wary of every form of authority, from the police to city representatives. The sale of food is changing; even in large, typically Anglo supermarkets, you can smell tortillas cooking. Dozens of Mexican radio stations dominate the airwaves, with some featuring *narco corrido* music, which celebrates the drug runner. One of the most popular names given to newborns in California this past decade was José. And new businesses are springing up to serve the market for quinceañeras, coming-out parties for fifteen-year-old girls.

There are many other changes in Fresno as well. The local university is changing its course offerings to reflect the new demographic. Decision makers on the city council are paying attention to new interests. The vast sums of money from the local economy that are flowing back to Mexico are starting to be noticed by economists. Advertisers have discovered the vast Hispanic market; now I drive down streets in Fresno where billboards are all in Spanish.

The Virgin of Guadalupe has been declared the patron saint of all of the Americas, and many are anticipating her five-hundredth birthday in 2031.[5] On that day, North America in general, and Fresno in particular, will begin to understand how thoroughly migration has altered the look, the sound, the feel and the very definition of what it means to be an American. As *The Economist* reported, the Census Bureau forecasts that by 2050 "the Hispanic population will have increased by 200 percent, the population as a whole by 50 percent, and whites, only 30 percent."[6] Immigration policy is now a hot national topic. In Fresno, migrants just organized the largest demonstration in the city's history.

Massive movements of people are a fact of life in a globalized world, especially a world characterized by huge disparities in wealth and security. The gap between rich and poor in my state has never been wider.[7] It is well documented that the movement of whole people groups to cities is spurred by push factors, such as economic instability, war, famine and loss of land;[8] and pull factors such as jobs and health care in cities, and their net effect on the movement of people groups, is also well documented.[9] Each week, the cities of the world grow by a net one million people.[10] It has been noted that China must now build twenty cities per year of one million or more people just to handle the massive rural-to-urban migration taking place there.[11] The infrastructure of Calcutta, with sixteen million residents, is already being stretched past the breaking point; each day the city "breathes in 3 million additional day workers, and exhales them at night to just beyond the borders."[12]

Here in North America, immigrants stretch civic infrastructures while also playing a vital role in cities. While the controversy over illegal immigration blazes, some cities actually court immigrants because they are seen as "an elixir for faltering urban economies." This help for urban economies is the byproduct of a combination of

> sheer immigrant energy with globalization, the Internet, satellite communications, ease of travel, enabling people from vast areas of the globe to connect and transfer information and

money and engage in borderless commerce. Among some immigrant groups the rate of entrepreneurship is two to three times that of the U.S. population.[13]

Today, more Mexicans live in Los Angeles than in any city of Mexico, with the exception of Mexico City and Guadalajara. More Cambodians live in Long Beach, California, than in the Phnom Penh, Cambodia. More Filipinos live in Daily City, California, than anywhere outside of Manila. Fresno is the Hmong capital of the world outside of Laos, and central California is the center of Sikh life in the United States. A major portion of the two-million-strong Indian diaspora to the United States is located on the west coast of California. And immigration is defining what it means to be young in America today. According to the recent Urban Institute report, 22 percent of all U.S. children younger than six have immigrant parents.[14]

But, of course, immigrants are not always welcome. They are grudgingly tolerated when they provide labor and services that U.S. citizens will not perform. As they move into more desirable jobs at the lower end of the economic scale, such as janitorial services, low-income, non-immigrant citizens complain. Yet so needed are these immigrant workers (estimated at eight to ten million), that sweeping overhauls of U.S. immigration laws have been proposed, including the creation of a new temporary worker program to "legally match immigrant workers with U.S. employers."[15]

THE FORCE UP-CLOSE

Even if you are an observer of these remarkable changes, unless you've had chances to interact with and experience the changes, to a large extent their impact will remain hidden to you. To really see and understand change, one has to be in the midst of it, to taste it, to experience it. I have had the privilege of sitting in the homes of immigrant neighbors—Mexican, Laotian, Hmong—and I am finally beginning to understand how profoundly and comprehensively migration influences a city.

Our neighbors, the Ramirez family, work the fields and several service-sector jobs. Their 950-square-foot home provides shelter for seventeen of them. Only two of the seventeen have proper documentation. All but the children work. Situations like this one are repeated thousands of times in Fresno. The money these immigrant family groups spend shopping for basic necessities alone pumps millions into our local economy.

Even though the Ramirezes work exceedingly hard, they spent their first two years in that home without a source of heat. They live a cash existence, do not benefit from banking or credit, often forgo medical treatment and live life looking over their shoulders. The only reason the reality of economic immigration is shaping my life is because two of the Ramirez kids, Hector and Ruby, come to my house for tutoring. It's only because I have squeezed into a living room with the seventeen people living there, eaten carne asada and listened as they told of risking their lives in the desert. They responded to the economic magnet of *el norte,* the north, to do jobs no one else wanted. They are being tolerated but not welcomed for the services they perform. In their shoes, I would likely have done the same. To them, Fresno—even much-maligned Fresno—is a blessing.

CITY AS SAVIOR

Cities are blessings to the poor—even cities thirty-two times larger than Fresno. The reason the poorest of the poor in India clamber to the already overcrowded city of Calcutta, which strains under the burden of grinding and dehumanizing poverty, is because they can buy a meal there for four rupees (about eight cents). The city will sustain them. As historian and theologian Ray Bakke observed, the Scriptures equate the city with the goodness of God and his steadfast love toward his people as they wandered in the desert.[16] As "they cried to the LORD in their trouble," the city was his answer to their prayer (Ps 107:1-7).

Living in a migrant stream has helped me uncover the ways that the city is an answer to prayer. As Paul addressed that distinguished gathering on the Areopagus, in the urban heart of the Greek world, he reminded them that it is God who has "made all nations [all ethnic groups] to inhabit the whole earth, and he allotted the times of their existence and the boundaries of the places where they would live" (Acts 17:26). Because we believe in a sovereign God who by his will causes or allows the movements of people across the earth, we can have confidence that the hand of God is active in this process. That same text provides further insight into what he might be accomplishing through urbanization and the internationalization of cities. It says "he allotted the times of their existence and the boundaries of the places where they would live, *so that they would search for God* and perhaps grope for him and find him" (vv. 26-27, italics mine). There is something about the dynamic of whole people groups in motion that creates a spiritual longing and a thirst for God. People intuitively gravitate toward the city in their vulnerability. And in God's design, this has something to do with their search for him.

12

When Things Boil, Things Rise

Life in the neighborhood turns normal vision into x-ray vision. Over the long haul, it becomes easier to see beneath the surface of things and find the origins of the forces at work in a city. But a measure of this vision can also be acquired during short, intense exposures to that city. These intentional experiences act like a new set of lenses.

Paul and Silas demonstrated this in Philippi (Acts 16:11—17:1). Paul's missionary journeys took a decidedly urban route, focusing on the crossroads of language and culture and commerce.[1] In Philippi Paul conducted a short-term mission lasting only a few days (v. 12). While there, he and Silas engaged in several levels of ministry, with each level providing experiences that led to the unmasking of spiritual forces. These experiences included relational ministry with Lydia, an affluent businesswoman (vv. 14-15),[2] and confrontational, liberational and spiritual ministry with an exploited and possessed slave (vv. 16-18). They included public proclamation in the marketplace, the "center of public life,"[3] and redemptive suffering as Paul and Silas were accused and beaten (vv. 22-24). They included general prison ministry and witness (v. 25), individual witness to a civil servant and his family (vv. 29-32) and intentional influence of the criminal justice system to ensure its integrity (13:7-39).

Now think about this: Even that quick summary of Paul and Silas's experiences in the city reveals the way a relatively short, intense experience can identify forces that influence specific outcomes in a city. The gospel addressed those forces. For example, it revealed the *spiritual void* and subsequent *hunger* among the affluent of the city—a readiness for spiritual things that is so often the outcome of secular life and the experience of those disappointed by the empty promises of the pursuit of money. It also revealed the presence of *exploitation* in the city, the manipulation of the most vulnerable people for economic gain. It revealed the power of businessmen in the city to contort and coerce the political process to serve their own ends as they brought Paul and Silas before the judges. It revealed the power of *racism* in the city as these businessmen injected the ethnicity of Paul and Silas into the argument against them. It revealed the power of *state-sponsored violence* as Paul and Silas were beaten.

My friend Pastor Jonathan Villalobos told me about meeting a woman as he and members of a group were walking and praying in Lowell. As they stood in front of her rented apartment, she shared a very sad but typical story: She had saved for years to purchase a tiny home just down the street from us. As she was on her way to participate in the city's first-time homebuyers assistance program, where she would have to demonstrate that she had a sufficient down payment to begin, she met two men from the region of Mexico she had come from. They showed her bones they claimed were sacred relics, bones of saints that had been blessed in their home region and that had healing power. Because this woman's daughter was very ill, she gave these men a significant portion of her savings to purchase the bones. These men had exploited her devotion, and now she was not able to buy the house. The experience of following Christ in the city, even on a short walk, brings things to the surface, things that are obvious to the vulnerable but that the outsider often can't imagine exist.

Without the onramp that these experiences provide, trying to minister in the city is like attempting to run across a freeway. You are likely to be broadsided by forces moving like invisible trucks. But experiencing them, even through short events, helps reveal the forces we must contend with, and helps us merge into the flow of what God is doing to address those things that prevent the well-being of those he loves.

13

Sins of Omission

If I exploit you, manipulate you, discriminate against you, avert justice in your case, as the slave girl and Paul and Silas experienced in Philippi, it is obvious to you that a force has been initiated against you. But the poor often experience another kind of force, one less obvious but just as potent.

The Hellenistic widows in the Acts 6 narrative were simply forgotten in the chaos of dealing with the needs of a rapidly growing church in an urban context marked by conflict and famine. The act of not bringing them food, even as others were being cared for, was tantamount to saying, "You don't exist."

Neglect—the absence of initiative, of investment, of interest, of care—is as powerful a force as any we have described, shaping individual lives and entire communities. Many studies have examined how neglect has been a strategy of the powerful for economic gain in cities. Using the now illegal practice of redlining, banks ceased making loans to certain parts of the city (most often, the sections where minorities lived). The rich who controlled city services, such as garbage collection and policing, gave those communities less priority, thus negatively impacting the services in those areas. All this combined to decrease the value of those parts of town. Banks swooped in and purchased those properties at fire-sale prices. At that point they made new loans, and good city services mysteriously became a priority again in those areas. This resulted in huge profits for financial institutions. But the power of neglect had impacted every aspect of life for those residents caught in the cycle.

THE JOURNEY OF THE SHOPPING CART

These forces are well documented, but documentation rarely helps us understand. Instead I invite you to come with me as I follow one of the many abandoned shopping carts that litter the streets of Lowell. There's one parked on the alley today as I write this, just behind my house. As you come, I invite you to practice the reflection that is at the heart of experiential discipleship. Reflection goes beyond mere description to explore and enter the drama of what is seen. I hope you'll see how it marked *me*.

A man with gnarled, filthy hands grips the bar of the cart as I watch, sometimes pushing, sometimes pulling, sometimes barely holding on. He wheels it, not over smooth commercial tile, not down neat aisles of groceries, but rattling over cracked pavement, down graffiti-scrawled alleys. No more do smooth hands with polished nails skillfully navigate the predictable turns of the supermarket, filling the cart quickly with groceries. No more do chubby legs press against the flimsy seat and toothless gums soak the red plastic bar with warm and innocent drool. No, say hello to broken glass and cardboard and twisted metal. Aluminum cans and bottles blend with the remnants of their former contents—soda, wine, beer—dripping like a putrid cocktail through the lower cage to the street, a leaking trail of stench.

The homeless man guiding this cart's journey stops right there on the street to take a leak, then decides to take care of it all, to defecate against the building in this alley, in the shade of its overhang. He doesn't seem to care that he is seen as he squats. This community has neglected his dignity, and now so does he. When he finishes, he steps over a dust-covered condom thrown last week from the window of a car, which had been parked there while the business was accomplished, and once again grabs the bar of the cart to resume his journey. He tips over another can, getting by on the recyclable waste of the poor. I watch him lower his eyes as he passes someone while muttering strange, confused words about being tardy.

Seven-year-old Gerald watches as the cart passes, has in fact watched it all, standing behind the cyclone fence that casts a dappled shadow on his dirt yard. His half-smile reveals that his vision of what is "normal" has already been shaped. He does not know it. He processes his view of the world alone, the adults in his life neglecting to provide another model. Each time something has contributed to this sad "normal," he has been unaware of the change. When the neglect of an empty refrigerator at home is repeated for weeks, he learns not to depend on home to get his needs met. When the landlord doesn't fix the heater, he thinks this is what landlords do. When his babysitter is the television, which blares all day, he assumes this is how we know what is important. The adults in his life have given up that role. When the vendors come to the house selling Popsicles for twice the price charged by the grocery store, he squanders his money on them. The adults in his life have neglected to tell him that he could get two for the price of that one. When he looks up to streetlights that do not work, he passively accepts it. The city's neglect has shaped his expectations. When his streets are unswept by the city, neglected for more than forty years, he is not offended by the garbage. He throws it there himself. This is just how the streets are. This is his normal. It has been defining itself since his birth, and he has not known it.

Gerald runs to the porch and hides behind a cracked and peeling pillar to spy on the cart passing by. The edge of the roof held up by the pillar is crumbling because of a perpetual upstairs leak from a rusting evaporative cooler. Green moss and slime drip from the point of the overhang. It is the only green in the neglected yard.

The cart continues its rattle over poorly paved streets. The man pushes it into an ancient pothole and is stopped short, sending the contents over its edge. Dirt and gravel and trash make passage difficult. He curses, readjusts the load and returns to the broken sidewalk.

He passes Eternity, a little blond girl from our tutoring program. Her wide, hollow eyes blankly follow the man. She reminds me of Cosette, the orphaned girl in *Les Misérables*. Her frail, waiflike appearance and passive stare speak volumes.

I first met Eternity standing at the table in our large dining room. Twenty neighborhood kids were there, doing a Christmas craft. I surveyed the tutors who were helping and noticed that some of them looked troubled. One child had come to the club without having eaten the entire day. Another had been carried off by child protective services as the tutors arrived at her house to pick her up. And here at the table, a tutor was doing her best to stay close to Eternity.

I am used to the more troublesome smells of the city. Lice spray, unwashed clothes, urine-soaked pants, T-shirts that are slept in and then worn to school. But I was not prepared for the sickening smell of neglect that arose from her thin body. She smelled so bad I had to stifle the urge to throw up. All I could manage to do was hand her a paintbrush and say, "I'm glad you are here. Stay as long as you want."

This memory rattles through my brain in a flash as, silently, the man pushes the cart by Eternity on his way to complete his journey to the recycler. His anonymous story is like those of dozens who travel down my alley, one of thousands in the city.

REFLECT!

God never intended for people and their environments to be neglected. The dirty street, the broken sidewalk, the leaky roof, the lonely child, the dusty condom, and the sad and hollow eyes are as accepted and unseen by the majority as the man who steers the cart. They are mere brush strokes in a portrait of neglect. Neglect of people and places shapes the way the neglected view themselves and the world.

Places matter to God, whether entire cities or simply a section of a town. Scripture takes note of places, gives them names, ascribes spiritual lessons to them, calls us to remember them. Theologians call this a theology of place. It is the simple recognition that human history takes place *on location;* the drama of people relating to God is anchored to a time and space on the earth. Jesus often used physical places to convey spiritual truths, whether referring to the architecture of the temple in Jerusalem (Mt 24:1) or to the urban tragedy of a tower falling on city people (Lk 13:4). Places matter because they influence the rhythms and realities of our lives, shape our values, and contribute to our identities.

Like an old painting found hiding in a walled-off space in the attic, some things can be uncovered only by demolition or dismantling. The experience of following a shopping cart was that for me. The significance of such fresh views of forces at work in the city and their relationship to my life in Christ can be determined only by closer examination, reflection and some initial steps of response. A discipleship that responds to experience by engaging in reflection and by formulating a course of action has the power to mobilize God's people to address the forces in the city. This cycle is the very thing that drove me to get involved in helping to assess the housing needs in Fresno through a citywide survey and in engaging the church in the current housing crisis. It drove me to be part of a coalition to help get our neighborhood streets paved and get streetlights on the alleys. It's the thing that motivates me to jump up and down and wave my arms if necessary to say to the city, "This neighborhood matters!"

14

Hosea's Excruciating Assignment

THE RIPTIDE FORCE AWAY FROM GOD

Some things can only be seen through pain. Invisible, intangible forces become apparent when circumstances are raw enough to sensitize the soul.

It had been an awful experience for God to love the nation of Israel, the nation that from the year 722 B.C. had in every way prostituted itself and forsaken its identity as God's own. God commanded Hosea to, in the words of Bible expositor Derek Kidner, "do the last thing a responsible prophet might expect. 'Go marry a prostitute . . . because this is exactly what I, the Lord, have married in pledging myself to all of you.'"[1] Hosea's marriage to the prostitute named Gomer was a *symbol* that dramatized not only the nature of Israel's unfaithfulness but also the consequences of that unfaithfulness. As we read that story we witness in stark human terms the negative fallout in Hosea's marriage, his new wife's adultery and the children of calamity who were born to them. The kids are named for violent cities (Hos 1:4) and for the abandonment Israel would experience from God (1:6-9).

But why would God call Hosea to marry a prostitute and to experience the pain of her infidelity? Some background will help. The context of this dramatic story is the city, and in particular, the rebellion against God happening in the cities of Hosea's time. Cities are used as metaphors in the book of Hosea, symbolizing powerful forces, some that are obvious and others that are invisible to the average eye. For example, the city of Jezreel symbolizes violence (1:4-5). Gilgal and Bethel (nicknamed Beth-avel—"House of Evil") symbolize abandonment of faith in God and the worship of idols. Gilead and Shechem (6:8-9) represent evil-doing, theft, bloodshed and an "indictment of the whole nation,"[2] and Gibeah (9:9), a twisted depravity which "at that period was only equaled by its arrogance."[3] When cities are mentioned generally in the book of Hosea, their fortifications are symbols of rebellion, a force against God that will be judged (8:14).

Israel as a whole, including her cities, is condemned in the book of Hosea for deep-seated forces that characterize their *civitas*—their behaviors and practice—including rejection of knowledge and of God (4:6), lust (4:18), violence (6:8-9), injustice (10:13), idolatry (13:2) and the failure of leaders (13:10). These powerful forces act as an ocean riptide, pulling people away from God.

That the people in those cities engaged in these practices makes God's loving statements that long for restoration all the more poignant. God imagines the day when he will take Israel "for my wife forever; I will take you for my wife in righteousness and in justice, in steadfast love, and in mercy. I will take you for my wife in faithfulness; and you shall know the LORD" (2:19-20). He imagines a day when his people love him rather than merely appease him through sacrifice (6:6). He longs for the day when he can regain them, when they cry out to him from their hearts (7:13-14). The Lord actively calls them to return to him and to "hold fast to love and justice, / and wait continually for your God" (12:6).

NANCY'S PAINFUL/JOYFUL INVESTMENT

Why would God call Hosea to such a life? Weren't other prophets merely called to proclaim God's words to an unfaithful nation? Sometimes God calls us to a visceral experience in order to bring about change. He called my friend Nancy Donat to invest her life in a preteen girl named May over many years. She mentored May, pouring herself into the friendship. There were sleepovers, afternoons spent baking cookies, Bible studies. May accepted Christ early on and showed signs of a real faith. Nancy spent hours with her, helping her to process all of the painful issues and experiences of a young girl growing up in the 'hood. They laughed together and cried together.

As May grew into young womanhood, the pull of the neighborhood was too strong. She's currently living with her boyfriend, who is in a gang, is in control of her movements and is making her life miserable. She is not following Christ right now. Nancy feels—and experiences—May's alienation from God. Because she is so heavily invested in May's life, she sees firsthand the anatomy of how a young girl, so excited about her faith, gets pulled away from God by the powerful current of the neighborhood. She understands, in a way she never could have from the outside, the excruciating tragedy of a child of God being seduced away from her Maker. Nancy hasn't given up, but her hope is tinged with pain.

Hosea's unique call to experience on a personal level the drama of his nation's plight accomplished what mere spoken words could not, in at least two ways. First, it provided an unmistakable object lesson for Israel; this scandal must have been the talk of all the cities. Hosea's direct experience of painful obedience—his experiential discipleship—must have generated mass reflection on those forces that had led Israel down the road of debauchery and that threatened its very security as the dominant shadow of Syria was expanding toward it into what would be-come an overthrow.[4]

Second, Hosea's experience would have changed his approach to ministry, his passion for his nation and his personal commitment to renewal. We will not be able to commit ourselves to the transformation of the city if we have not experienced some of its pain. As Kidner notes, "It is the people you love that can hurt you most."[5] Perhaps that connection to pain will come from sitting with a woman who has just been beaten by her husband. Perhaps it will come from listening to a family who has just been evicted. Perhaps it will come from staying up all night helping someone detox or waiting up with an anxious parent for his wayward teenager to come home.

MANUEL AND KIM

Unlike Hosea, my friend Kim was not commanded by God to marry Manuel for the *purpose* of experiencing those forces. But the fruit of her marriage to him—someone who had lived in the riptide force away from God—was an up-close understanding of its power. Kim was a white, college-educated urban missionary. Manuel was Mexican, undocumented, with a history of gang involvement and time spent in jail for a felony. But Manuel came to Christ in jail, and Kim watched the utter transformation of the man. Over time he became a leading force for the transformation of the Lowell neighborhood. Countless young gang members came to Christ over the years as a result of his mentoring. As she watched Manuel minister to young men in the neighborhood, Kim saw with greater insight the pressures they lived under and the things that pulled them from God. I remember attending a funeral with her and Manuel of a friend who was in a gang. She spoke with deep understanding and compassion for the despair and hopelessness in the room, and she talked about the ingrained cycles of violence and the dying hope for liberation—all up-close insights she had gained about the pull away from God.

But she also saw God pull back—exercise his own force for good. This was evident in Manuel. As Kim reminisced with me recently, she said, "When Manuel was getting ready to be released from jail all those years ago and he wanted others around him to know he was a changed man, he simply said to God, 'You know I'm a changed man and I know I'm a changed man, but I would really like other people around me to know. If you could take these tattoos off my body that would really be great. If you don't, that's okay, but I would really like that.'" Kim told me, "The tattoos began to fade and he no longer has *any* of them! The guys from his former gang are amazed that he has no tattoos since they all had them done together at the same time." This and hundreds of other examples of Manuel's experiential faith won Kim's heart over and over.

Their six-year courtship—no one could accuse them of rushing into things—was cause for alarm for family and friends at first. They pelted Kim with questions: "Won't Manuel return to his gang life?" "Won't someone from his past want to come get him?" "Will he be able to provide?" "Has he ever threatened you?" "Isn't his lack of a high-school diploma a problem?" These questions revealed the stereotypes and lack of faith that limit the transformation God can apparently accomplish in a person's life. They are themselves part of a riptide pulling *the middle class* away from God. Kim's marriage to Manuel was by no means the same thing as Hosea marrying Gomer, but to mistaken middle class eyes, it *looked* like that. It had shock value, something that would eventually prove very fruitful.

Friends of Kim and Manuel who saw the quality of his relationships and ministry and saw the fruit of transformation in his life, understood and supported their decision to marry. That's not to say that

Kim herself didn't have some fear of the risk. She felt she was step-ping into a situation where her options in life might diminish. She wondered if they would be forced to move to Mexico at some point, if they might find themselves homeless and jobless. She observed the way Manuel was stopped and questioned by the police occasionally, simply because he was walking down the street in their neighbor-hood. Would they falsely accuse him one day of something and would she have to bail him out of jail? She says, "Sometimes, when I just thought about all the factors that were against us, I could hardly breathe. I even had some nightmares about ending up on the streets."

But now that Manuel and Kim have modeled a healthy marriage and ministry for several years, others are coming to them for advice on crosscultural, crossclass relationships. And Kim is marveling at the things she has learned from her marriage, things she could not have known without her connection to Manuel. Certainly this in-cludes insight into the gang and drug culture, which helps her in her ministry. But it goes beyond that, shedding light into human nature and power dynamics. For example, Kim says,

> I have been with Manuel around police, lawyers and others in the justice system as we have worked through neighborhood or immigration issues, and have watched the mature, confident man I am married to all-of-a-sudden *look* and *sound* like some-one who just got out of jail, instead of someone who has left all that behind more than twelve years ago. I have watched police stop him on the street and give him little lectures about staying clean and away from gang members. Now, I can't imagine living this way and being treated this way so many times and not wanting to retaliate. I learn grace from Manuel as I watch him handle these situations with a firm graciousness.

Other experiences have led to up-close insights about what a background of poverty and deprivation can develop in a person. It took a while for Kim to understand Manuel's practice of moving light bulbs around the house instead of buying more. When one went out in the hallway, he would simply move one from the bedroom. Then there's Manuel's open-handed compassion. When a car is stranded on the side of the road, he stops to help. When a homeless man's pants fall down, he stops and gently hikes them up. When a neighbor is out of gas, Manuel finds a few dollars to tide them over. Deprivation has spawned generosity, creativity and resourcefulness. Kim sees all of this up-close.

But the lessons go beyond what Kim and Manuel have learned personally. Their marriage speaks volumes. To middle- and upper-class friends, first it shocked, then gently, by example, it rebuked. To many of their friends in the barrio, it spoke of reconciliation, of new beginnings and redemption. Though there are huge differences between Manuel and Kim's story and Hosea and Gomer's story, in one major similarity their marriage has become both a symbol of redemption and a source of inspiration to a culture skeptical that real change is possible.

Hosea's experience of personal pain in the cities of his nation exposed the riptide forces that pull people from God, putting those forces on display for all to see. Hosea's experience of pain demonstrated—uncovered—what the nation should have been feeling. As Kim and Manuel crossed the lines of class and culture, their experiences in their marriage uncovered both inner-city realities and middle-class judgments that are part of that same riptide—in a way nothing else could.

15

Race Matters

THE FORCE OF RACIALIZATION

To expose what is hidden, sometimes someone has to get up in your face. Even a small confrontation can reveal things that have been obscured by privilege or position.

One midfall afternoon I was standing on the sidelines of my twelve-year-old son Jameson's flag football game on the Lowell elementary school field, surrounded by third- and fourth-grade classes, a few teachers and handful of parents. The sun was casting hard and clean October shadows. Jameson was one of only three white kids on the team; the rest were first-generation Mexican Americans. He was a head taller than those Latino boys. The coach had made him the quarterback, but I had to fight off a gnawing sense of embarrassment. True, he was good—probably a better QB than all those boys on the team who were new to American football. But I couldn't help feeling like he was another example of a white boy, albeit a "minority" in this case, rising naturally and effortlessly into a position of leadership. Was it just another example of white privilege at work? Or was I being oversensitive? The question put me off-balance.

I looked at the other team's bench. The all-African American team had come from Carver, another poor-neighborhood school. Their entire support section consisted of their coach, one mom and one dad.

The referee did not show up, so the vice principal of our school, a very professional-looking, light-skinned Hispanic was asked to officiate. He looks more Italian than Mexican American. One of the other white fathers on our team volunteered to assist the vice principal in refereeing the game. I was asked to hold a timer's watch. On that day I was wearing nice slacks and a white shirt with a button-down collar. My cell phone dangled from my belt.

Halfway through the game, the mom and dad on the other team were questioning every call, stepping off yardages, arguing with our "referees," questioning the clock. It didn't help that our team won the game in the last five seconds by a touchdown thrown by my son. The other team exploded. The parents and players accused us of cheating. They wouldn't shake our hands. They wouldn't cheer, "Two, four, six, eight, who do we appreciate?" They didn't appreciate us.

The angry mom from the opposing team looked at me with disgust and said, "We get this everywhere we go. Unfair treatment by you people." I was instantly wounded, like so many white people are when they feel misunderstood, feel unfairly judged, feel that they are not being treated as individuals but instead as part of some generalized racial group. Of course, these are the feelings people of color have felt for generations. My automatic posture as a white person, the posture I often default to under pressure, is a purely individualistic, relationally oriented understanding of what constitutes "racism." So often, I and many of my white friends are unable, due primarily to our individualistic approach, to recognize the systemic and institutional dimensions and realities of racism and therefore are incapable of proposing solutions at that level.[1] We cannot imagine a system could be inclined against a sixth grade football team. We cannot imagine what it feels like to doubt the system at every level.

The pain of the accusation created an ache in the pit of my stomach. In a moment of defensiveness I wanted to shout right back at her, "How dare you question my integrity! How dare you think I would trade my dignity for a few seconds on a clock!" even though I wasn't absolutely sure I had run the clock perfectly. I felt self-protective and embarrassed in front of the kids, in front of my son. But I managed to say, "What do you mean?"

"Look who held the reins of power in this game: a partisan team of white referees and a white timekeeper whose son was throwing the winning touchdown," she replied. She looked at me and I felt at that moment that she must be sick and tired of explaining it again. Sick and tired of being sick and tired. Tired of the racial issues that were wearing everybody out at the school as Southeast Asian, Latino, African American and white parents drew battle lines. Mournful for her boys, whose self-image was far too affected by wins and losses, who had to live always conscious of the way the deck was stacked against them.

At that point I decided to play the clergy card, the "I'm an exception" card. I said to her, "Ma'am, I just want you to know that I am a minister. I couldn't live with myself if I didn't keep an honest clock. I don't doubt that you have had unfair treatment other places, but here you got an honest game. I just wanted you to know that."

At that she grabs my hand and said, "You're a believer too? Well, praise the Lord." She smiled and told me what church she went to. She asked me about mine. She was relieved, but not much. She'd be at the next game, she said, the next school. And there, it was "unlikely a pastor will hold the timepiece." The shadow of doubt would follow her team wherever they went. The exception only proved the rule.

The issue of race and the level of racialization experienced in the city skews and influences every human interaction there. A racialized society is a "society wherein race matters profoundly for differences in life experiences, life opportunities, and social relationships."[2] Entering into, understanding and—to whatever extent possible—experiencing some aspect of the pain caused by this is a key strategy to uncovering the reality of racism's force in the city. As author David Shipler has noted, "Racial issues confront the country on three levels, public policy, institutional, and individual, and at each one, the response is now a curious coexistence of intensive effort and cold neglect."[3] Experience in the most daily and mundane aspects of life in the city—football games, PTA meetings, convenience-store purchases—unveils the degree to which racial issues infiltrate the fabric of life at each of those levels. That experience forces a choice: will we make an intensive effort toward reconciliation and solidarity, or will we settle further into cold neglect?

To ignore or live in denial of the centrality of race and racial issues in the heart of the city is to miss a key onramp of understanding. Because our ethnic appearance is the first piece of information people take in when they meet us, because this is a racialized society and because we are made in the image of God, those who would try to make a difference in the city must not miss this onramp. To do so is to relegate your discipleship and even your noble ministry efforts to little more than a frontage road in the kingdom of God, perhaps paralleling the freeway for a while, but never merging onto the transformational journey God has for every disciple. The point is to go with God, not just to go. And the point is to go where God is going, not just to be out on an excursion. God's shalom highway leads to the place where his image is clearly visible on every face, shining with the knowledge of that fact. To miss the signals of race means even the best-intended attempts at bringing transformation in the city will be shortsighted, short-lived and ultimately resented.

16

So Many Choices

Anyone paying attention knows that crosscultural mission no longer requires crossing an ocean. In the city, it often requires just crossing the street. Cities are internationalizing. Harvard professor Juan Enriquez has noted that of the 150 or so flags of nation-states in existence today, more than 75 percent did not exist fifty years ago. Nation-states are fragmenting, often by culture and ethnicity. Because of migration and globalization, cities now have become catch basins of culture, an amazing blend of tastes and aromas simmering together to create an urban stew. Diverse religious practice is part and parcel of the fabric of urbanizing society. And cities are fertile ground for spiritual movements.[1] If I take a walking tour of the three-block radius around my house, I can see implications of religious pluralism. I can watch a chicken being sacrificed to dedicate a new playground while listening to the chanting of a Hmong shaman. I can walk past a shrine in a neighbor's yard to the Virgin of Guadalupe, encased in Plexiglas and lit at night. I can listen to the loudspeaker of the Pentecostal church beginning its summer revival series. And I can watch turbaned and bearded Sikh men drive by on their way to the new temple.

The powerful force of religious pluralism in the city means that those who attempt to have a gospel-inspired transformational influence there struggle with the question of how to retain a commitment to the truth and uniqueness of the Christian faith without alienating those of other beliefs. Indian theologian Paul Swarup puts the question well: "How does one avoid compromise on the exclusive claims of Jesus Christ, but at the same time be involved together . . . in a common program for establishing justice, peace and the transformation of lives?"[2] My three-block walk teaches me that we must find a way to "become cultural pluralists without being religious pluralists,"[3] as longtime missionary to India and missiologist Lesslie Newbigin put it.

Our experience in Lowell has helped us develop some examples of what that might look like. First, we have committed to do everything openly as Christians. We do not hide or camouflage our faith. Lowell elementary school sends children to our Wise Old Owl Tutoring Program, though it knows it includes Christian songs and a prayer at the end. We do this while openly respecting aspects of the faiths of the children we tutor.

Second, we never make a commitment to faith or its practice compulsory. The songs and prayers at the end of tutoring are optional and voluntary.

Third, we look for ways to partner with local efforts sponsored by any agency doing something that is obviously worthwhile. We might send volunteers, help to organize an event or publicize something.

Fourth, we build real relationships with people of other faiths and no faith. If we are invited to participate in an event we can't agree with, the strength of those relationships gives us the ability to decline the invitation without cutting off further ties and opportunities for witness.

Fifth, we focus on what is central—the lordship of Christ—rather than on more peripheral doctrines or differences in church practice.

Unfortunately, many urban churches have opted for a privatized form of faith that never engages other religious systems and, worse, either refuses or passively neglects opportunities to work alongside people of other faiths for the common good of the community.

The diversity of cultures in the city and the deep ties between a person's religion and his or her culture means that Christians who are committed to transformation in a community must develop a broad and diverse set of skills to operate in this pluralistic context. We need the ability to build collaborative urban networks, working alongside people of other faiths or no faith. And in that process we need the ability to remarry evangelism and social action, which went through a divorce in this country in the 1920s, during the growing fundamentalist-modernist controversies.

Working alongside people with different religious traditions than our own, or no religious tradition, has taught us that this is possible. Developing a shared experience of service in the city creates a platform for authentic sharing of faith. In one case, an openly anti-Christian man with whom I had worked on a project in the neighborhood told me that I was different from all the other Christians he had met, which led to an opportunity to share my faith. To my amazement, he made a point of leading a prayer at a subsequent community meeting. On another occasion, the daughter of a nominally Catholic woman with whom we have repaired dozens of roofs and porches in the neighborhood decided to return to church because of the influence of that activity and the friendships that evolved during it.

If we ignore the force of religious pluralism in the city and assume that a one-size-fits-all gospel message will work when we design evangelistic outreaches or attempt to do church planting, we will be disappointed. All it takes is one chicken with its head cut off and a shaman chanting Buddhist prayers to realize instantly that one methodology does not fit all.

17

Eating Kitty Litter

THE FORCE OF INNOCENCE

We have been looking at how experience in the city can unveil invisible forces at work that, like gale-force winds, can shape life in powerful and often destructive ways. But it's also true that experience can reveal those things in the city that act like stakes in the ground—an equal, opposite, positive force to hold against the wind. My experience on an urban experiential discipleship project helped me see one of these forces—these stakes—at work for the first time.

We had invited about fifteen college students to live and serve in Lowell. They spent a week building relationships with children and youth, as well as doing painting and cleanup projects. The culmination of the week was a special evening of fun designed to be a creative outreach to teenagers in the neighborhood, many of whom were affected by gangs, drugs and family brokenness, and some of whom were the cause of the brokenness.

As we sat down to plan the event with Brenda, the youth worker in charge of teen outreach at the inner-city mission that was hosting us, she suggested a format: We could have stations through which groups of teens would rotate for periods of five to ten minutes. Each station would offer something different. *So far so good,* I thought. But then she suggested that we use a "playland" theme, or something of the sort.

"Wouldn't it be fun," she said, "if at each station was something a five-year-old would enjoy? For example, what if at one station we put Tootsie Rolls on a square bed of granola, called it 'kitty litter' and suggest that the group eat it. What if another station was 'story land,' where one of your leaders will read a picture book to the teens seated in a semicircle, just like kindergarten. And what if another station was 'dress-up land,' where we have a bunch of old clothes and a mirror and let the teens play dress-up, and then take their picture? And what if a station involved games like Ring Around the Rosy and Mother May I? Wouldn't it be fun?"

Are you nuts? I thought. All I could imagine was a group of sullen teenagers, bored to tears, rolling their eyes and saying, "This sucks." In my inexperience, I said, "Brenda, I'm not sure about this. It seems like it could be a big flop."

She replied, "It could be, but of course that will depend on you. If you think it's stupid and won't work, then it won't. But if you have fun with it, they will too."

And that's what happened. Teenagers from this neighborhood with the highest crime rate, the highest drug use and the worst poverty streamed into the room and within five minutes had embraced the theme. At the first station a college student named Shiela Skibbie was reading the children's picture book *The Three Little Wolves and the Big Bad Pig* to a group of mostly young men. I recognized some of them as being from College Avenue, the home of a local division of the Bulldogs gang. To my amazement, they were listening attentively as Shiela read the words and showed the pictures. Every once in a while, she would ask a question about the story and insist that the "children" raise their hands in order to answer. This they did eagerly, and in voices that mimicked a five-year-old's. I shook my head in disbelief and moved on to the next station. There I found teens in floppy hats, dresses (not always on girls), and suits and ties, posing for group pictures. Our students were assisting in the process by applying lipstick and helping with accessories. They handed out Polaroid shots to all the teens who participated. Elsewhere, big, tough-looking boys were singing, "Ashes, ashes, we all fall down."

So many of these young people had seen awful things in their lives; they'd grown up too fast. I had assumed that this meant they would be insulted by this childish stuff. But in their chaotic world, where all of the adult options were available to them, they were starving for a chance to be kids again.

Emboldened by the success of that evening, the following year we threw a party for five teens, all of whom had overcome incredible barriers and were ready to graduate from high school. Shiela, by then on staff with our ministry, suggested, "Wouldn't it be fun if we placed certain baby foods, such as Gerber's Split Peas or Mashed Yellow Squash into the bottoms of Pampers disposable diapers, gave one to each teen and had a contest to see who could eat theirs first?" I didn't even bat an eye.

The laughter and enjoyment of those teens was so loud, so sustained and so pure that I am sure it is still echoing somewhere in the universe today. They speak dreamily of that day as some of the most fun they've ever had. Innocence might be covered up, but apparently it is a force for good that can never be taken away.

Who from the outside would guess it, as they speed by in their cars, escaping neighborhoods where muscular teens with multiple tattoos plant themselves expressionless on urban street corners? Who would believe they would eat baby food and listen to *The Three Little Wolves and the Big Bad Pig*? Only those who were there to experience it.

Epilogue to Part 2

In 2 Kings 6 we read of an attendant of the prophet Elisha who got up early in the morning and went out in the city of Dothan. To his dismay, he found the city surrounded by the forces of the king of Aram, an enemy of Israel bent on killing the prophet. Alarmed he reported their hopeless situation to Elisha. The calm response of the prophet must have seemed otherworldly to the attendant. It pointed to an invisible reality that was greater than the forces arrayed in front of them. He prayed that the attendant's eyes would be opened to see the heavenly forces in their midst, forces that though invisible would be more than enough to be victorious. At that, the attendant's eyes were opened and he saw "horses and chariots of fire all around Elisha" (v. 17). Furthermore, Elisha never had to use those armies of God to defeat the enemy. He enlisted another force instead. He prayed that the enemy would be struck with blindness, and then he led them peacefully to the city of Samaria, where he spared their lives.

In part two we have focused on just a handful of the forces that are shaping the lives of the poor in the city, including a city's identity, migration, neglect, racialization, pluralism and even innocence. We have seen the power of experience to uncover these forces and help us understand them. Seeing them up-close can be daunting. And it's easy to forget that we require the hand of God when trying to engage the forces. It is a spiritual task at its heart and requires spiritual force to bring solutions.

THE FORCE OF PRAYER

Remember Zorro—I mean Raymond—who was talking to my tree? The forces of addiction and mental illness seemed to be the only powers at work in his life—until one morning at three, when he frantically began pounding on our front door. I went downstairs in my pajamas. When I opened the door, I saw he was dressed in filthy jeans and a T-shirt. I liked the cape better. He said, "Father, father, I need your help."

Raymond always called me Father. I guess I fit the image of a priest, the only category he had for a sincerely religious man. I had corrected him many times, saying, "Raymond, I'm not a priest; I just love God." But it never registered. He would begin his confessions: the drinking, the fights, the girlfriend, the UFOs.

Raymond had been sleeping in the field next to our house, having missed the curfew in the board-and-care home where he lived. Gang members from around the corner had tried to mug him. We called the police and waited. After twenty minutes we decided to go back out to the porch to flag them down. After twenty more minutes and no police, we decided to go to the edge of the street and sit on the curb to be sure they wouldn't miss us.

So there we were, Zorro and the pajama priest, sitting in the gutter with water running under our feet. I remember thinking, *This is ridiculous. There are three gangs in this neighborhood, and this is the witching hour, the worst possible time to be sitting on this curb. And besides, what the heck do I know about how to relate with Raymond? What can I give to him? He's addicted; he's mentally ill. Culturally, the gulf between us is too great. These forces are too big for me. I have no training in this. Before I* knew it, these thoughts had turned into a prayer for help.

And so we sat, waiting for the police as I prayed silently for God to do something. The police never came, and after a while my thoughts about the forces working against Raymond and against the neighborhood became too great. I was just getting ready to say to Raymond, "It looks like they're not coming, and I need to go back in," when he leaned into me, like a tired child. And in a moment of rare lucidity, he said, "Father, would you pray for me?" Prayer. Yes, that was something I knew how to do. If I didn't have the solution for Raymond's addiction, for his mental illness, for the gang members who plagued the neighborhood or for any of the multitude of other forces arrayed against the dignity of people who live here, at the very least I knew how to pray. And so I did, right there in the gutter. We said amen, and Raymond decided to see if he could crawl back into his board-and-care home through an open window.

A few days later, Raymond knocked on my door in the middle of the day. He was sober and speaking rationally. He still called me Father, but this time he asked for a Bible. That was his only reason for stopping by. Priests often have Bibles, you know. It seems there are some forces, hidden like Elisha's angels, that are more than enough for victory. It took sitting in a gutter to uncover them.

PART 3

Onramps and Speed Bumps

STEERING TOWARD

TRANSFORMATION OF THE CITY

18

Personal Transformation That Leads to Community Transformation

There's a bumper sticker I see from time to time, usually on cars that have more than one. It says, "If you're not outraged, you're not paying attention." Somehow, somewhere, it became acceptable—even regarded as inevitable—in my city, that nearly four out of ten children live under the federal poverty line, that 38 percent of the population is food-insecure (the food budget runs out before the end of the month), that fewer than one in five households can afford a median-priced home, that we have the worst school system in the state, that we have the worst air in the nation, that we have an average of 15 percent unemployment and that we have the highest teen-pregnancy rate in California. Not only are many of us in the church *not* outraged at these social realities, but also we have so individualized and internalized our faith that it has become disengaged from social systems altogether, in effect becoming "privately engaging but socially irrelevant."[1] We have so wrapped our faith in comfort and equated it with an innocuous niceness that we can't imagine it compelling us to become disturbed, or for that matter, disturbing. We can't imagine allowing anything to disrupt our lives, certainly not involvement in the complexities of community transformation.

Our "faith" doesn't require it, even though the apostle James reminded us that the truest expression of faith is "to care for orphans and widows in their distress, and to keep oneself unstained by the world" (Jas 1:27) As Oxford theologian N. T. Wright laments,

> Plenty of people in the church and outside have made up a "Jesus" for themselves, and have found that this invented character makes few real demands on them. He makes them feel happy from time to time but doesn't challenge them, doesn't suggest they get up and do something about the plight of the world. Which is, of course, what the real Jesus had an uncomfortable habit of doing.[2]

Fact is, the majority of us are pretty embarrassed by people who are so passionate about certain issues they seem to have no other life. And we are rightly horrified by those who let their passions over specific issues such as abortion or homosexuality lead to acts of violence. If outrage leads to that, then we're happy to carry on our quiet, private lives of faith. We may feel a twinge of guilt or anxiety when faced with seemingly intractable urban problems, such as homelessness, poverty, illiteracy, hunger, gang violence and substandard housing. But it's as if we have made a decision that, because we can't go around in a perpetual state of outrage, we'll enter what writer George Simmel has called "an urban trance": "We can deal with the anxiety generated by the homeless who sleep on urban streets or starving Third World peasants by simply not focusing on them."[3]

The more positive and proactive cousin of that bumper sticker calling us to be outraged is from the prophet Amos, who cried out, "Let justice roll down like waters, / and righteousness like an everflowing stream" (Amos 5:24). Yet even as we affirm that majestic command, we are reminded that it's one thing to say it, but quite another to do it, to "work out the irrigation system," as pastor, theologian and activist William Sloan Coffin said. Only recently have evangelical leaders in the West begun to recapture what early Christians intuited: that we can wholeheartedly commit ourselves to Christ-motivated social action combined with the proclamation of the gospel without feeling we are somehow abandoning the "real" gospel for a "social" gospel.[4]

This legitimization doesn't mean the practice has trickled down to the church pews, where it is still assumed that Christian growth has to do primarily with internal or attitudinal changes. We hear a Scripture verse, such as, "[We] are being transformed into the same image from one degree of glory to another" (2 Cor 3:18) and assume this must refer merely to some interior character quality. We hear that we are not to "be conformed to this world, but be transformed by the renewing of your minds" (Rom 12:2) and assume that the goal is merely a change in our thinking. We hear that we are to "aspire to live quietly, to mind your own affairs, and to work with your hands" (1 Thess 4:11) and assume it's permission to be solely focused on our jobs, our families, our lives. Many believers can't imagine what theologian and activist Melba Maggay means when she calls us to "recover our prophetic voice, that agonizing howl all through the centuries against anything that demeans or debases people, that note of discord in the false harmony of an unjust status quo."[5] They don't like to think of becoming discordant, nor can they imagine how they might organize their lives in order to maximize their efforts toward kingdom transformation.

What is transformation, anyway? When speaking of our own transformation earlier in the book, I likened it to metamorphosis. Our context for this transformation has been the city. But it would be a mistake to presume that this means the city is only a "laboratory" for bringing personal change in the life of a disciple. Theologian Reinhold Niebuhr said, "Transformed people can transform a society."

The cycle of experience, reflection and application is itself generative, that is, it has a life of its own that can lead to social change. As we engage in the kind of ministry that has the potential to bring transformation to a community, the effect on us is more than a desire for personal growth. This is what Brazilian educator Paulo Freire called "conscientization . . . the process by which learners [disciples, to use Jesus' term] 'achieve a deepening awareness of both the sociocultural reality which shapes their lives and of their capacity to transform that reality through action upon it.'"[6] Our own transformation makes us avenues of transformation in the city.

Zebras and Other Unlikely Miracles

There are things that at first glance make no sense, but have perfectly sensible explanations. The herd of zebras grazing on the hillside outside my window right now is an example of this. If I were in some parts of Africa, it would stand to reason that I should see zebras out my window. But I am on a vacation at California's Central Coast, in a condominium. Out the front window are sailboats and tourists, SUVs, surfers and strollers. Out the back are golden foothills covered with black-and-white striped visions of Africa. There are ten of them, close enough to hear my whistles and looking completely at home. The sensible explanation: they are the leftovers from the Hearst Zoo, donated to the state and now roaming free and routinely stopping traffic on Highway 1.

A few weeks ago I saw something that also made no sense. Some two hundred college students had returned from spending their summers living among the poorest urban dwellers in the world in Calcutta and Bangkok, among the scavengers in the garbage villages in Cairo and on Smokey Mountain in Manila, in ministries of compassion and solidarity connected to a specialized InterVarsity program called the Global Urban Trek. On their return over thirty of them dedicated themselves to spending at least two years in ministry among the urban poor while investigating the possibility of longer-term calls. I watched them as they knelt before candles in prayer for some of the people they had met during the summer, dedicating themselves in various forms to seek their shalom. They looked like a newly formed monastic movement.[7]

Now, I can understand why students go on typical short-term mission trips. They have good intentions, they go with their friends, they bring many of their Western comforts with them, they know they can do some good, and then they return to "normal." But why would a student pay to live in a garbage village or in a shanty washed away routinely by putrid floods, where their tidy views of God and their Western expectations and privileges are dismantled? Those students who knelt at the post-project debriefing were saying no to the American dream of upward mobility, of acquisition and consumption, and of success and security. And they were not alone: over a thousand students each year participate in domestic urban projects sponsored by InterVarsity that place them in ministries of compassion and justice in the poorest and often most violent neighborhoods of the United States.[8] On the outside this picture makes little sense. But there is, in fact, a very sensible explanation. *Transformed people gravitate toward exercising a transformational influence on their surroundings.* What does transformation look like? Let me tell a few stories.

SNAPSHOTS OF TRANSFORMATION

Paul participated in an urban experiential discipleship project in Detroit. During that year he met Wayne Gordon and John Perkins as they spoke in Detroit about Christian community development. Paul told me, "God used InterVarsity to begin shaping my vision and love for inner-city ministry, while Coach Gordon and Dr. Perkins along with others fueled it." After further reflection sparked by a seminar on inner-city ministry at the Urbana Student Mission Convention, Paul went on to pursue church-based ministry in the neighborhood with some of his peers in InterVarsity. Since then, some of those peers have gone on to direct the Detroit urban projects.

While substitute teaching after graduation, Paul prayed and sought the Lord about his future. He accepted positions in Michigan and Washington, D.C., that involved various community service projects covering five states. This journey eventually led him and his new wife to the Lawndale neighborhood in Chicago, which has been characterized by neglect, burned-out buildings, drugs and despair for thirty years. They joined Lawndale Community Church, which is faithfully and creatively ministering there.

When I ran into Paul, he was serving at the Lawndale Community Development Corporation as comanager of the Lawndale College Opportunity Program. This ministry prepares high school students from the neighborhood for acceptance and success in college. In addition, he and his wife have fallen in love with both the community and the ministry and have relocated to Lawndale, where they are purchasing a home. Paul credits the presence of "wonderful men and women of God in our lives that God has used to shape our vision and love for the city." Their intent is to stay there for the long term, consistently providing new options for young people, contributing to the stabilization of a once burned-out community, working toward the transformation of the neighborhood and seeking its peace.

Joyce, an alumna of an InterVarsity urban discipleship project in Jackson, Mississippi, has served as the vice principal of Circle-Rock Preparatory School, part of Circle Urban Ministries in Chicago, and most recently as administrative dean for the middle school and as a literature and language arts teacher. Her goal of providing quality, affordable education to children in Chicago's Austin community is part of a plan to develop future servant leaders for the neighborhood, to raise those leaders for individual and community transformation through the power of the gospel.

They have seen a tremendous response to their work already. Children are receiving a higher-quality education than they would receive in the local, distressed public school. They are gaining access to cultural capital, to experiences that broaden their horizons about their life and the world (for example, participation in ballet, vocational instruction in classical music, interactions with adults from various ethnic groups). Joyce is having a measurable transformational influence on her city, an influence that is shaping the way community members experience life.

Theodora was a young believer involved in International Fellowship of Evangelical Students (IFES) on her university campus in Uganda, which regularly engaged in works of compassion. After joining the staff of that movement, she created a ministry to a slum community that provides food, school fees, vocational training and health care to over three hundred children. She chose that community because that's where the IFES ministry office was, and her choice turned out to be strategic. Alumni of the same student ministry who went on to be doctors now come regularly to serve at the clinic.

When Theodora noticed that many of the community's children had gone on to college and were themselves involved in a student ministry, she instituted a college scholarship program that requires graduates to come back to serve. Because of the food provided at class each week, nutrition in the wider district has improved.

This program, called the FOCUS Child Development Project in Uganda, is still running after many years and is part of the fabric of student ministry there. The transformation is widespread and measurable as both college students and children are impacted.

TRANSFORMATION AND CHANGE

To say a community is "transformed" does not mean all need is erased or all conflict overcome. It is not a state that a community *arrives* at. Every community is made of individuals whose personal sin has clear ripple effects in the lives of others. For that reason, it's best that we speak of community transformation as an ongoing process. As Indian churchman Richard Howell noted, "Transformation is not changing what is, but creating what isn't."[9] He is referring to things like job opportunities, new housing, new social relationships—new levels of shalom. This type of transformation is important because every community has institutions whose very systems and ways of operating have been founded on greed, expanded through exploitation or embedded with oppressive values.

Certainly revival in those systems can "change what is." Communities have experienced comprehensive, historic transformations through revivals, as happened during the Welsh revival of 1904, when the bars and brothels in those cities closed for lack of business and judges announced empty dockets. But even there, a generation later, deeply embedded sin patterns reemerged and new ones developed.

Change is inevitable. Human systems are in a perpetual state of entropy; they are fragmenting and decaying at all times. New communities built to house low-income people become slums, and urban renewal projects designed to bring revitalization are eventually overshadowed by destructive forces like drugs, which cause an exodus from the city to the suburbs. Later, communities that had once been poster children for urban decay become attractive again to those seeking affordable housing, and gentrification takes over. Banks and real-estate agents manipulate and accelerate this process at times, a well-documented phenomenon in this country's history. Whatever the cause, whether it be genuine revival leading to positive social change or greed-based manipulation leading to social upheaval, communities go through cycles of decline and repair.

THE HALFWAY POINT

So where does transformation fit in this cycle of decay and rebuilding? Transformation includes repair, but it is more than that as well; it is the creation of something new. We will know a community has crossed the halfway point in transformation when access is created for everyone, including its most vulnerable members—access that meets their needs and develops all aspects of their humanity. This is how great cities are to be measured. Do all of its people have the opportunity to know the love of their Creator and be part of a fellowship of love? Is the dignity of work available to them? Can they feed, house and clothe their family? Will they be able to access health care that they can afford? Can they be included in all voluntary associations? Are ample opportunities available to improve their lives? Will they receive fair treatment and equal justice? Can they contribute to the well-being of others? A community is being transformed to the extent that it can say yes to these realities for the majority of its residents.

At its core, transformation means that residents are experiencing increasing measures of shalom. *Shalom* is a Hebrew word often translated as "peace." But as a principle, it is so much more expansive than the mere absence of conflict. As Martin Luther King Jr. said, "True peace is not nearly the absence of tension, it is the presence of justice."[10] Shalom can mean justice, righteousness, well-being, prosperity, the flourishing of all that God has created in all of its interrelatedness.[11] Because shalom is translated into all those words, sometimes the average person reading the Bible doesn't know that it's the same word in each case and therefore can't grasp just how broad and comprehensive shalom is.

As mentioned in chapter seven, shalom is best defined as making things as they *ought* to be *for* people, *in* people and *between* people.[12] When a city takes care to make things as they ought to be *for* people, it means that the people can meet their most basic needs for provision and security. When the people of a city have shalom *in* them, it's likely that the city and especially people of faith in the city are taking care to ensure that the dignity and moral uprightness of its people are fostered and protected. When the people of a city experience shalom *between* them, it usually means that key leaders in the city are taking pains to facilitate that process, because it rarely happens on its own, especially when race and class divisions prevail.

Transformation means the development of shalom. This is why we contend that those followers of Jesus who want to have a transformational influence must look beyond service to reshaping the systems of the city in ways that help a city say yes to the questions asked above. If we are to contribute to the transformation of the city, even as we are being transformed, we must link our activities to those kinds of goals.

The church has played key transformational roles throughout history. Ray Bakke, called by many a modern-day apostle to the cities, recalls that the sixteenth-century Reformer John Calvin assigned some of the deacons of his church to monitor the hospital in Geneva to ensure that the poor were receiving adequate care; this led to the transformation of health care. Bakke tells us in his book *A Theology as Big as the City* that Christians in first-century Rome routinely retrieved bodies from pits called *carnarii,* where Romans threw their dead captives as well as the carcasses of animals. These Christians gave them decent burials, leading to the transformation of social mores. In the second century, female leaders of the church in Cairo retrieved abandoned infants from alleys and back roads and brought them to the public square where they sat under pagan statues and acted as wet nurses to them, saving their lives while sending a clear message to the populace of the city of the contrast between Christianity and pagan culture.[13]

SAME MESSAGE, DIFFERENT MILLENNIUM

That same message is being sent today, leading to transformation. In Lowell, Nancy Donat bought a house after spending a year learning about urban ministry through InterVarsity's Fresno Institute for Urban Leadership. Her time in that program, coupled with previous incarnational ministry experience, transformed the way she saw life, her skills and privileges, and her sense of purpose in the world. Nancy is a nurse by training, and she has integrated her nursing skills with the relational connections that only an involved neighbor can achieve. She advocates for neighbors who are struggling with health issues, connects uninsured people to health resources and works with the school to put on health fairs for residents. She even sponsors a prayer booth at these fairs. Nancy also converted the second story of her home to a special room used for tutoring, Bible clubs and play—a fun, safe and meaningful place for neighborhood kids.

Nancy's influence is felt daily, and the difference she has made at the school is measurable. The director of the Neighborhood Resource Center trusts her and gives her much freedom to work in the school, despite the fact that she is a missionary with International Teams and often represents Bethany Inner-City Church in her neighborhood work.

Nancy's acts of service are more than service. They are leveraged—increased in the transformational nature of their impact and effectiveness—because she intentionally connects them to institutions in the neighborhood. This increases the capacities of the institutions, making the institutions and the neighborhood itself more sustainable (able to sustain balanced, healthy rhythms), even while under relentless social pressures.

It Takes a Student to Save a School

Sometimes this kind of ministry does even more than boost sustainability. Sometimes it is responsible for plucking institutions from the jaws of annihilation. The students of an inner-city charter school in Tampa had just failed a schoolwide charter test. If they failed a second test, coming up in a few months, the school would lose its charter. The principal had taken over the failing school with hopes of turning it around, but the hurdles seemed too great and the time too short. When he discovered that InterVarsity students were tutoring children in the neighborhood on a regular basis, he called Brian Sanders, an InterVarsity divisional director and resident of the neighborhood, asking if the students could conduct a series of Saturday schools to get the kids ready for the second test.

Brian said yes and focused the efforts of his students on the task. To the principal's amazement and joy, the school children passed the charter test. The InterVarsity students were gratified to know that their efforts had not only saved the school but also boosted the teachers' morale. The school would go on to face other challenges, foremost of which was financial viability that would prove insurmountable, but the neighborhood itself had learned a transformational lesson about what the investment of a few key individuals could produce. The teachers and administrators at the school will use that transformational model to address whatever assignment they find themselves facing down the road.

THE HOUSE JANET BUILT

Sometimes a small investment leads to big transformation. On an urban experiential discipleship project in St. Louis, Janet Stevens was helping to repair the roof on a Habitat for Humanity project. As she swung her hammer, her reflections on homelessness inspired her to pray about what she might do to address the problem in a more holistic manner. She returned to school at George Washington University (GWU) the following semester, still praying about what to do. Her major was architecture, and to her amazement, she discovered that the School of Architecture at GWU and the city of St. Louis were sponsoring a design competition. Student teams would be given twenty-four hours to design a home that was aesthetically pleasing but affordable to low-income people. The city would build the design of the winner of the competition.

Janet quickly assembled a team of her classmates and produced a design they felt proud of. They entered their design—and won. As a result of Janet going beyond the project's immediate goals, the city of St. Louis now has an innovative, efficient, environmentally sensitive example of an aesthetically pleasing, financially accessible home for low-income residents. And Janet has discovered that her skills can be applied not only to fix a leaky roof for a single family but also to literally transform the way a city cares for the housing needs of its most vulnerable residents. This is transformation.

One of the more amazing outcomes of the power of experience in the city is the way one small action on the part of someone who is experiencing transformation can play a strategic role and, in fact, provide a "hinge" moment on which future transformations hang. In

InterVarsity's Los Angeles urban project, one student began to care deeply about young men involved in gangs. His concern grew greater than his fear and he began to befriend a young gang member. The young man eventually came to Christ, which, to the student's surprise and amazement, led to the dismantling of the entire gang. Other young men in the gang came to Christ, which had a ripple effect in their families and friendships. Other gang members watched this process, which influenced their lives as well. A community was freed from some of the harassment perpetuated by gangs. This kind of transformation is the gift that keeps on giving.

Another student on the same project (but during a different year) became concerned about the presence of a corner liquor store that was playing a prominent and even aggressive role in the addiction and despair of a certain neighborhood. This student's process of transformation led to him relocating to just a few houses away from the liquor store. That relocation opened his eyes even more to the unlawful and even evil impact the store was having. Eventually he began mobilizing neighbors to pressure city leaders to remove the store's liquor license. City leaders agreed that the store was violating multiple laws and removed its license. This student's role in the process and his open allegiance to Jesus were well known on the street. The gospel had compelled him to make the community's problems his own, and his actions changed the way the community experienced life. This is transformation.

TRANSFORMING VISION

Our point can never be simply to give people a service experience in the city, though that can be a perspective-changing event in itself. It can never be simply to educate Christians about the need for compassion in urban America. And while there is merit in giving a cup of cold water in Jesus' name, the more far-reaching and compassionate act is to make sure that an "irrigation system" is in place so that justice can "roll down like waters, / and righteousness like an ever-flowing stream" (Amos 5:24).

We've all heard the adage "Give someone a fish and he'll eat for a day; teach someone to fish and he'll eat for a lifetime." But the question John Perkins continually poses is, "When will we ever get to the place when it becomes normative for us to ask, 'Who owns the pond?'" In other words, how can we focus our efforts in such a way that the poor of our city can experience a life that is sustainable and self-determining? We need to keep our eye on the goal of transformation, looking past the immediate act of service to larger potential outcomes as we orchestrate experiential discipleship programs, outcomes that contribute to a measurable metamorphosis toward a broad shalom, where everyone can own a piece of the pond.

NORMAN'S POND

Norman just came by my house. This solid, twelve-year-old, African American boy wanted to show me a trophy he was given for his participation in a summer martial arts class at the neighborhood community center. I asked him to show me some of the moves he had been learning, and he was glad to have an audience. I was happy to hear that Norman was enrolled in an activity; when he is bored, he stirs up trouble. We've had to make it clear to him many times that his aggressive behavior during our tutoring program is inappropriate. Even with those stern admonitions, he keeps coming back. Will Norman have a piece of the pond? Does experiential discipleship have the power to help facilitate that kind of vested ownership for the next generation?

Fifteen years ago, if you had described my life and ministry in

Fresno today, I wouldn't have believed you. In fact, I might have been overwhelmed and run screaming into the night. What got us here? I trace this journey back to a single experience. While on sabbatical in Oxford, England, before having anything to do with urban ministry, we met urban missionaries from a squatter settlement in Manila. They were New Zealanders, also on sabbatical in Oxford. As new friends do occasionally, we compared photo albums. Theirs showed their life in Manila, where they lived in a shack with cardboard walls and a corrugated tin roof. Open sewage flowed down the center of their dirt street. Their children played with cardboard boxes while surrounded by adoring Filipino adopted grandparents. The couple talked of their work doing church planting, sanitation projects, literacy programs, microenterprise development—all sorts of transformational ministries that were bringing change to the slum community where they lived. Our photo album showed our children in the hedged and clean world of suburbia, surrounded by the latest electronic toys, coated with insulating layers of affluence.

I remember saying to our new friends, "You must be amazing people to do what you're doing." They had undoubtedly heard this reaction before, and in their thick New Zealand accents, they responded with something like this: "Nah, Randy, we just found where Jesus lived and moved in with him." That phrase rattled around in my soul for months, coming up again and again in conversations with our friends.

When we returned to the States, we initiated our first urban experiential discipleship project, which took college students out of their safe and insulating environments on campus and placed them with agencies having a transformational influence in cities. As we applied the things we learned in that setting from year to year, we found our lives being reoriented. Each year we added components to our program: a ministry training center, two tutoring programs, additional urban projects, multiple learning environments and, most important, thousands of interactions and experiences in the city.

Now, fifteen years later, we are ready for Norman when he arrives at our door, his eyes bright with excitement over his achievement. His life is being transformed in so many ways: He's learning to read through the help of our tutors, which is, even as I write this, altering the trajectory of his life. He's learning to relate across lines of class, race and age. He's learning how to modify his behavior. And he's hearing about Jesus, who has the power to change the streets he walks on, the family he's a part of, the house he lives in and the very options available to him as he attempts to avoid the negative future just about everyone ascribes to him. Norman will transform into a young man soon, and I believe he is on his way to owning a piece of the pond. As that happens he will become an agent of transformation as well.

19

Speed Bumps

Sometimes we must intentionally place speed bumps in the path of participants when we create an experiential discipleship onramp in the city. Speed bumps on an onramp? This seems to fly in the face of logic, doesn't it? Aren't we supposed to be accelerating? In their well-intentioned enthusiasm for being agents of hope and conduits of practical help among those who are poor and marginalized, young leaders often rush ahead with plans or actions that can have an opposite effect from what they intended. Sometimes the first command must be to slow down, wait, make sure you understand the flow you are trying to join.

Speed Bump #1: First Do No Harm

Hippocrates was a Greek physician who lived more than four hundred years before Christ. He is best known for the Hippocratic Oath, which still guides the medical community. The phrase "first do no harm," attributed to the oath (but more likely coming from another document, *Epidemics*[1]) is one of the most fundamental principles in medical ethics. When a physician seeks to help an individual, at the very least the procedure the doctor uses must not make the patient worse. The cure must not be worse than the disease.

On one urban experiential discipleship project, students met a child in an afterschool program who had no socks. After the program that day, they stopped by Wal-Mart on their way to drop the child off at his home. The socks cost very little, pocket change to the students, and they gave no thought to what they felt was a small, compassionate act. When they got to the child's home, they explained to the mother what they had done, and she became defensive and angry. She had been humiliated that these students felt she could not afford socks that cost $1.29. Their supposed act of compassion had done harm to this woman's dignity and increased the gulf between the students and the mother, making a relationship all the more difficult.

On another project, students agreed to paint the home of an elderly resident in a decaying neighborhood. For the most part, they did a good job, but they left it unfinished. In addition, they had spilled an entire gallon of paint on the walkway and not cleaned it up. The initial gratitude on the part of the resident began to evaporate as the months went by with the job unfinished. The mess left on the walkway was a permanent, ugly scar, reminding the now bitter resident that this was no more than a "project" to the students, something that helped them feel better about themselves; and he was forgotten when it was over.

On another project, a participant assigned to volunteer at an agency that reached out to the homeless began to lose interest in the third week of a six-week summer program. She was hot, she missed her boyfriend, and she was having interpersonal problems with some of the other participants on the project. Her attitude turned sour toward the agency personnel and toward the homeless clients who came there for services. The agency director expressed dismay at her attitude and contacted the project leader to say he was doubtful they would want volunteers from that group for the next year.

We often attract young leaders to experiential discipleship projects in the city who, by virtue of their lack of experience, are prone to make blunders that can bring harm. If those who lead them focus on bringing change only in participants' lives, they forget to consider the negative outcome of such mistakes in the lives of the people they minister to. It's impossible to anticipate every "worst practice" or to avoid making unfortunate and hurtful mistakes, despite good intentions. And it is impossible to catalog them all here. We could examine the damage done by the well-meaning student who promises she will "come back to visit" a child, but then forgets as the new term at college begins. We could explore the psychological damage to a community when a "needs survey" is done for the tenth time in two years by various groups, but nothing ever comes of the data collected. We could reflect on what happens when a group breezes in and creates a temporary ministry program that goes off with a bang but leaves a gaping crater when it is over and the group leaves.

Groups wishing to participate in transformational ministry in the city without bringing harm must set into place a process of orientation that identifies specific things to be cautious over. We can try to anticipate potential mistakes, but, more important, we must put a mechanism in place that will help us to work together to overcome the blunders when they inevitably happen. This mechanism is simple and can be included in any experiential discipleship event in a city. It is composed of three basic elements: (1) When faced with decisions about how to minister in planned activities, involve participants in a communal process of prayer and discernment. Ask your ministry host to help your group plan an activity. (2) Expose participants to the insight and guidance of a local agency, church or leaders when faced with unplanned dilemmas or questions. These are teachable moments when local expertise means the most. (3) Formulate an action plan that initiates repentance and an invitation of reconciliation when offenses occur. The words "Help me understand what we did wrong and how we could change it" go a long way in repairing the breaks in relationship that occur when ministering across cultural or class contexts.

This initial speed bump—"First do no harm"—is as much about preparing for inevitable harm as it is about avoiding it.

Speed Bump #2: Check the Map

We don't slow down for anything these days while driving—not to dial numbers on our cell phones, not even to eat. I recently saw a guy driving a VW on the freeway, holding a burger in his left hand and a drink in his right hand, chewing the French fries sticking out of his mouth (I don't know where they came from) and steering with his left knee. I also can't tell you the number of times I've seen someone driving while consulting a map, spread out over the steering wheel, looking up only every five seconds or so.

We can't be careless like that as we orchestrate experiential discipleship in the city. It's crucial to orient ourselves properly toward this journey. We need not just to slow down, but also to pull over and consider where we're going. If a deliberate process of preparing participants for the context in which they will serve—checking the map—is not in place on our way to the city, it's time to get out of the car and postpone the trip. Anything less than serious preparation represents a callous disregard for the city.

The nature of the orientation we craft will change, depending on things such as the context of the event or project, its length, the nature of the interactions we are orchestrating or the ethnic makeup of the team or host community. But a good starting place is the determination to help participants be ready to encounter differences, especially those defined by class, race or culture. We want to help them assume a posture for entering a specific urban neighborhood that inclines them toward real transformation and helps prevent the importation of judgmental attitudes and actions that might bring harm.

Duane Elmer and others have worked collaboratively to produce an excellent description of the way a person's posture when entering into crosscultural encounters determines not only whether their experience will be positive or negative, but also the quality of their impact and the level of transformational influence. In various forms, this diagram (see figure 1) has alternately been called the Entry Posture Diagram, the Cultural Adjustment Map[2] and the Approaching Differences Diagram. Elmer and other missiologists discovered that when we are thrust into an environment radically different from our normative culture, whether it's in a developing country or an inner-city neighborhood in our own country, the result is often frustration, confusion, tension, embarrassment, misunderstanding and aggression.

You can enter into crosscultural differences with one of two postures. The desirable attitude (often depicted in the diagram as a green line) is characterized by *openness* to new things, *acceptance* of the cultural distinctives one is encountering, *trust* that things will work out and that your welfare will be cared for, and *adaptability* to strange customs or ways of doing things.

The undesirable posture (often depicted in the diagram as a red line) is characterized by *suspicion* of people's motives or abilities, *fear* of differences, *prejudice* or *superiority*. Regardless of your chosen posture when entering into these differences, there will always be a measure of frustration, confusion, tension and so on. But your entry posture can determine your choices about how to deal with those results. As seen in figure 1, those who enter with openness, acceptance,

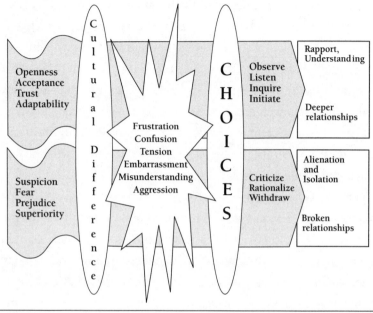

Figure 1

trust and adaptability have an easier time choosing to *observe* the new surroundings, to carefully *listen* to what people mean, to *inquire* about things they don't understand and to *initiate* relationships. Those who enter with suspicion, fear, prejudice or superiority most often choose to criticize things they don't understand in their new surroundings, rationalize explanations of blame and end up withdrawing, either literally going home or retreating emotionally and not engaging. Each choice has typical outcomes. Those who choose to observe, listen, inquire and initiate often find themselves developing rapport and understanding; they keep relationships in their mission context. Those who choose to criticize, rationalize and withdraw often find themselves alienated and isolated; they many times leave a trail of broken relationships in their mission context.

The act of "checking the map" might involve walking participants through the cultural adjustment model before they begin their service in the city and then revisiting the figure a few days into the project. As participants experience the inevitable difficulties that arise in crosscultural settings, leaders can identify teachable moments when an interaction has exemplified either a "green line" posture or a "red line" posture. Participants often pick up on this metaphor and spontaneously help hold each other accountable by saying, "You're red-lining right now."

The act of checking the map doesn't have to be limited to the orientation before the journey. Sometimes it's best to stop in the middle of an urban discipleship project and reproduce some measure of frustration, tension, embarrassment or misunderstanding typical of any journey involving crosscultural situations, through the use of simulations or games, many of which are available online.[3] In one game called What's New? an intentionally unjust society is constructed based on the number of syllables in each person's name. The more syllables, the more power the person has in that society. Many of the rules in that society are set up to their advantage. I have seen this game played all over the country, and the inevitable results include normally privileged people *feeling* for the first time what it's like to be at a disadvantage, normally excluded people *feeling* what it's like to be in power, normally law-abiding people *feeling* the need to disobey or circumvent the rules and solid individualists *feeling* the need to work with others toward community solutions. It's just a simulation, but the feelings are real.

Another simulation involves placing one person outside a group while that group decides on a form of communication designed to direct the excluded person to perform a culturally appropriate behavior or task. It might simply be clapping in unison. When the excluded person enters the room, he or she must determine what the group wants him or her to do, with only the clue of clapping to go on. He or she must use trial and error, must work through feelings of frustration about the lack of communication, must be willing to be embarrassed. Of course, all feelings must be discussed and debriefed.[4]

The act of checking the map, that is, getting ourselves ready for transformational ministry in the city, requires us to slow down long enough to look at the roadworthiness of our vehicle as much as the route we plan to take. Orientation and game-playing are the equivalent of checking the tires and the oil, and making sure we have the fuel to get us where God is leading us.

SPEED BUMP #3: INVENTORY THE ASSETS

In the movie *Apollo 13,* the astronauts must make it back to earth in a damaged space capsule, and they are running low on oxygen. To make matters worse, one of the filters designed to clean carbon dioxide out of the air is broken. If they don't come up with a solution fast, they will suffocate. In response, the cool-headed commander in Houston asks them to make a list of every item they have onboard so his engineers know what they have to work with. Eventually the engineers come up with a solution involving duct tape, packaging and miscellaneous parts assembled in a way that works well enough to repair the filter and get the astronauts home. The problem was obvious, but the solution wasn't, until someone took stock of the *assets* they had onboard.

Communities are like that. The obvious problems glare defiantly at us. Poverty, crime, drugs, illiteracy and more—all seem overwhelming, threatening and intractable. We spend an enormous amount of resource and energy in municipalities or through the social sciences cataloging neighborhood problems, surveying residents as to the problems, drawing media attention to the problems, raising money to address the problems. Those of us who design experiential discipleship projects or events in the city can easily fall into these approaches. It's understandable. Followers of Jesus want to meet needs. As the apostle John wrote, "How does God's love abide in anyone who has the world's goods and sees a brother or sister in need and yet refuses help?" (1 Jn 3:17). But rushing in to meet a need we think we've identified often ends in failure because the need is misidentified or misprioritized, or because the solutions proposed are not sustainable because they don't originate in a community or involve indigenous leaders.

Author and activist John McKnight articulated an approach to community development that can guide designers of urban discipleship programs toward more fruitful ministry. His asset-based[5] approach requires us to do what the Houston commander did with his astronauts: take stock of positive assets in the community that can be supported, built on, networked or leveraged for transformational impact. This approach begins "connecting them with one another in ways that multiply their power and effectiveness, and [begins] harnessing all those local institutions that are not yet available for local development purposes."[6] These assets include elderly anchors in the community, artists, disabled people, youth, both welfare recipients and the employed, as well as institutions and associations. They include the individual capacities of residents and local associations, organizations and institutions that can be focused on the rebuilding of the local economy.

As we plan urban projects that involve service, we should expend some effort in understanding the natural assets of a community or neighborhood and then link our plans to strengthening those assets. Perhaps it's a grandmother who lives on a corner in the neighborhood and cooks for half a dozen of the neighborhood kids. Perhaps it's a coach who has been at the local elementary school for thirty years and acts as a father to many boys. Perhaps it's a small business that routinely hires young people from the neighborhood for their first job. Perhaps it's a city staffer who runs homeownership classes at the neighborhood resource center. McKnight suggests that no matter what the category of asset, a four-fold strategy should be employed. We should (1) identify the capacities or assets we can see, (2) inventory the assets and resources of the community, (3) put this information into the service of mutually beneficial partnerships, and (4) on the basis of those partnerships, build new relationships with resources external to the community. As we identify assets and link our projects to them in ways that strengthen and encourage the work, our efforts become transformational.

I've seen the opposite of this too often in what is the normal approach to "serving the neighborhood." Energy is expended in ways that become swallowed by the overwhelming need and even by some of the pathologies of a neighborhood. For example, a month ago the police sponsored a neighborhood cleanup in Lowell. Thirty couches, twenty mattresses and dozens of tires that had been dumped illegally in the alleys were cleaned out by police, residents and church volunteers in a one-day community service project called a "Day of Caring." We were all grateful for the attention and that the dangerous and hazardous substances had been removed. But now, one month later, the alleys look the same. All that effort, and little to show for it. It's like walking a half mile to a corner store, buying a forty-two-ounce soda for your brother and arriving home to find it mostly gone because of a hole in the cup.

The act of identifying a neighborhood's assets can be an incredible service to churches and agencies trying to make a difference there for the long haul. In one San Antonio experiential disciple-ship project, director Jon Parker assigned some of his students to spend their entire summer surveying the community, not for its perceived problems but for its assets and its perceptions of local churches and agencies active there. This helped inform decisions the church was making about the nature of its long-term ministry in the neighborhood. Students went door-to-door, collected data, helped to collate it and then presented it in a report to the church, which transformed their plans.

This speed bump reminds us that first impressions rarely communicate the whole picture of a community and that we must slow down to fully comprehend the beauty, dignity and strength that is present in even the most marginal communities. We must slow down long enough to find out what the community has to offer, not just what it needs. It reminds us to craft our project in such a way as to support and nurture the assets already there.

SPEED BUMP #4: NO QUICK FIX

It seemed like such a good idea. Our neighborhood is dark at night. Drug deals and prostitution thrive there. Gang members and wan-nabes lurk in the shadows. The coalition of ministries focused on Lowell heard that Christian community developers from Detroit had plans to install globe lights in the front yard of every house in a neigh-borhood targeted for revitalization. It sounded like a great strategy. We chose Calaveras Street to become our showcase of change.

As we went door-to-door, offering the lights, we were met with a mix of skepticism and cautious openness. We felt there was a sense of ownership growing, though we'd realize later it was mostly among us in the coalition rather than among the neighbors. In fact, owner-ship was so high among coalition members that two groups argued about which one owned the project. Two brochures were produced, each claiming credit.

It began to take shape quickly. A church graciously donated money and found a pool of Christian prisoners on supervised work release to provide the labor. A local electrician was signed up to do the installation and a few kids from that street got to act as his apprentices. The project began with energy. It was something we could point to, an accomplishment; we were doing something.

But then the electrician broke his leg, and the project stalled. The parts needed to finish the job rode around in his car for the next year. Neighbors showed disgust that a promise had been made and then broken. It was only their disgust and our guilt that brought things to completion two years later. As the lights finally went on, we told ourselves they were important for both practical and symbolic reasons. We waited for our neighbors to rejoice with us, but they didn't. Some owners of apartments and a few longer-term residents felt that we should have selected lights compatible with the architecture of the neighborhood. Some wondered aloud whose responsibility it would be to repair the lights and replace the bulbs. And in a neighborhood with an annual turnover rate of 60 percent, many of the original residents who gave their okay to the project were long gone.

A few months later I drove along Calaveras Street at night. In the past it was the Wild West of my city, with drive-by shootings and an atmosphere of intimidation day and night, but especially night. (*Calaveras* is Spanish for "skulls.") It is better now. But that night as I drove down the street, only fourteen of the fifty-eight lights we had installed were operating.

Globe lights were not the neighbors' idea. The decision to install them was not the result of a neighborhood process. In the end we brought nonlights. We imported shadows, devices that not only didn't work but also brought an empty hope. Our enthusiastic efforts actually made our ministry harder on that street; it would take time to rebuild trust.

The painful lesson we learned from this experience was that we should never import solutions from the outside. Even very good ideas, if they are done without the partnership, insight and ownership of residents, will likely be done in a way that is not appropriate for the context or sustainable over the long haul. An imposed blessing is rarely a blessing at all.

In contrast, the play space in the backyard of Lowell's Neighborhood Resource Center was the brainchild of the center director and several residents and parents of Lowell school children, who were enlisted in the process of building. Bob Dittmar, the trusted director of All4One, a program of a local faith-based nonprofit, arranged for donations of materials and was enlisted to oversee the building of a playhouse and low bridge. Neighbor Joanie Martin designed murals for the fences, and neighborhood kids helped to paint them. It stands today as a testament of the resources of the community and is cherished and valued as a new asset for the blessing of countless children.

This speed bump reminds us to temper our enthusiasm, call into question the "obvious" diagnosis and prescriptions we give to a neighborhood's problems, and avoid the temptation to default to anything that resembles a quick fix.

SPEED BUMP #5: NO CHARITY

As a new believer, Pa Houa was proud to be part of the youth leadership team at a local ministry. Her parents were two of thousands of Hmong refugees who had spent ten years in a refugee camp in Thailand after fleeing Laos. After years in the camp, they had made it to America, settling in Fresno. Pa Houa was born in that camp, but as a child growing up in Fresno she quickly took on an American persona while navigating the cultural gap between her parents and her new environment.

On the leadership team, her role was to join with the other youth to help welcome suburban groups coming to her urban neighborhood to serve. High school groups from suburban churches came every summer to paint houses, put on Bible clubs and carnivals for children, and spread the gospel. This was her first time being involved in one of these projects.

To welcome the first group of the summer, they all sat in a circle and shared their names and favorite ice cream flavor. The leader of the suburban group suggested they pray. Brenda, the leader of the neighborhood ministry, told me that what happened next changed her understanding of ministry in the city forever. One by one, the mostly white, middle-class high school students prayed that God would help them "bring Jesus to the poor people who have to live here." They prayed for God to anoint their efforts "because most of the people living here are from bad families or are addicted to drugs." Most of the kids simply prayed that God would make them a blessing to "the poor" who lived here. Brenda said she watched Pa Houa open her eyes in the middle of those prayers and saw the realization dawn on her face that these kids were talking about *her* family, *her* friends and *her* neighborhood. She was "the poor" that they had come to "reach."

Pa Houa came to Brenda after the group left that day. She was crushed and furious that these students had come with a superior attitude. She didn't deny that her neighborhood was in serious need, but she had thought that they would be working in partnership, as equals. She decided not to be involved, and for years this insult was left unresolved in her mind. She had no interest in working with white, middle-class Christians any further.

Attitudes like the ones demonstrated by the suburban group that day are deeply entrenched. Influenced by socioeconomic assumptions and middle-class standards, they are rarely examined closely. This isn't surprising: The way we recruit participants to "service projects" is by stressing how "needy" the people are. We put pictures of grateful people receiving charity on our recruitment brochures, which appeals to the desires of a well-fed church to be benevolent. This act only strengthens the idea that we are entering this mission to "give." But as historian Michael Oleska said, "There is no one-way mission. To proclaim the gospel, to celebrate the truth, to reveal the kingdom, is always to establish a relationship between those who proclaim and those who hear that message, and both are changed in the process."[7]

It is incumbent on those of us who orient emerging leaders for transformational ministry in the city to help them see the city differently than they would on their own. Rather than allowing them to look at residents of an urban neighborhood only as potential recipients of the gospel, we need to help them consider the possibility that some of these neighborhoods produce a deep, warm and fertile pond of Christian and pre-Christian spirituality. We must help them consider what might be learned from the residents there and what it is that God might want to do in their own lives as a result of relating to people who are different, people who have to trust God for things they take for granted, people whose faith is experienced differently, dramatically and often in pragmatic and even miraculous ways.

This in no way suggests that those in the middle and upper classes have nothing to give or that they should not give what they know they have. It simply reminds us that giving is not the whole picture, that we are trying to establish transformational relationships. Transformational relationships bring change to both parties, opening our eyes to new dimensions of faith, opening doors of opportunity, giving birth to new prospects for community partnerships. Transformational relationships cannot be one-way.

That experience shaped the way Brenda prepared future groups for service. After she shared what happened to Pa Houa with another ministry group, she noticed members guarding their language, wrestling with their perceptions of the residents they were about to serve and being more careful to recognize others' dignity. She said that the process of considering the resident's potential shame caused them to reflect on the state of their own hearts. The result: increased humility.

This speed bump of recognizing that charity has the potential to be patronizing requires us to catalog our negative attitudes and perceptions and calls us to leave our judgmental mindsets at home.

LIFE ON A ONE-WAY STREET

I live just five blocks from the city center, on a one-way street leading out of downtown. I can see the freeway onramp from my porch. People race by at the end of the workday in a manic competition to get out of there, so there have been many, many accidents in front of our house. Someone should put in a speed bump.

One-way streets tend to increase speed and, unfortunately, carelessness. The same often happens when God's people engage in ministry in a city. We think we know the road, and we certainly know how to drive. We hardly think as we plan to pull off a ministry event. We call to rent the bounce house, arrange face-painting booths and a clown, get the fire department to come and spray the kids down with a fire hose. We recruit chaperones for the students in our group, arrange food and lodging for everyone, make sure to plan crazy games and fun into the schedule so they don't get bored. We do this all swiftly and efficiently because, of course, it has to fit in the context of all the other things we're doing as well. But we often don't slow down and check to be sure the car is ready and to be sure we are ready.

And every once in a while people surprise us by traveling in the opposite direction, people who either didn't *know* or didn't *agree* that the street was one-way. We honk at them madly, making all sorts of gestures to warn of the danger they are in. When someone like Pa Houa attempts to make the journey to the city a two-way street, it doesn't fit with the rules of the road in some middle-class minds. But if we expect the street to be two-way, we will likely avoid unnecessary accidents. Turns out, the rules for the driver are the same as for the physician: first do no harm.

Speed bumps are for slowing down. An interesting thing happens when we slow down: we start noticing what's around us. Instead of racing into the neighborhood to practice charitable acts of kindness out of context and racing home again when it's done, we hit speed bumps that cause us to recognize the nature of the problems we face and that there is no quick fix. Speed bumps cause us to notice the good things about the neighborhood, its assets and amenities that were a blur when we were traveling at top speed. We begin to see the raw material God can use to bring transformation that is sustainable, both in individuals' lives and in the whole community. And we begin to notice how, even on one-way streets, there is always two-way traffic, even if its pedestrians are walking against the flow.

20

Three Transformational Actions

Transformational Action #1: Know Your City

This is a test. How many elementary schools are in your city? Okay, not many people would know the answer to that one. But could you at least tell me where you would get the information? Not sure? What if I asked you how many churches there are? Not sure? Where would you get the information? What if those two questions could have a strategic relationship in the process of equipping God's people for transformational influence in your city?

Back in chapter nine we explored the concept that a city is made up of *identity markers*. The *urbs* of a city include major infrastructures that we take for granted, many of which operate invisibly. The *civitas*, the behaviors or relational networks in the city, are often even less tangible. The *anima*, the assumptions or beliefs of the people, operates as a silent, often secret backdrop informing everyday experience in large and small ways. This highly conceptual way of understanding our cities can help us imagine the physical, relational and spiritual ways the gospel might contribute to transformation.

Here we want to examine pragmatic ways of understanding a city, of getting to know it with the intent of creating onramps to involvement and transformation. The first way explores how various sectors operate in a city, how institutions in those sectors influence life in the neighborhood and how they relate with each other. The second way entails simple observation.

A trinity of institutional sectors. Every city is more than its geography. We can drive its streets for decades and still not understand how it operates, why things are the way they are, how things change or how the gospel can make a strategic difference in the way its residents experience life. But when a city is seen through the lens of its institutions, a picture begins to emerge that makes it clear how God's people can literally transform the experience of its poorest residents. One way to understand the role institutions play in a city and how they relate to each other is to think through the various sectors.

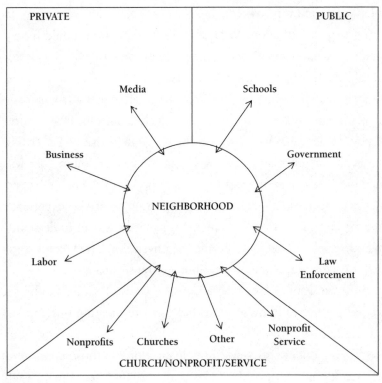

Figure 2

Reverend H. Spees, cofounder of One by One Leadership Foundation in Fresno, groups institutions into three sectors: public, private and church/nonprofit. (See figure 2.)

Once we have a visual grasp of institutional categories in the city, we ask several questions to help those of us committed to transformation know how to proceed. One we should ask is how a particular neighborhood experiences institutions in each category. A case in point: my neighborhood is named after the local school, Lowell Elementary. Using figure 2, I can ask, "What might the neighbors here think of the fact that the local school has the worst record in the school district?" I can ask, "How does the media characterize my neighborhood?" I can ask, "How do the residents experience the police here—as friends, as adversaries, as reliable, as respectful?" I can ask, "Are the local businesses seen as taking things away from the community or contributing to the community?" And I can ask, "To what extent would neighbors regard the church here as making a relevant contribution to people's lives in the neighborhood?"

Each of these questions, when coupled with our commitment to seek the things that make for shalom in a city, can lead to strategies for the involvement of God's people. For example, in affluent neighborhoods, residents hardly think about the departments at City Hall responsible for garbage collection or code enforcement because there are relatively few problems associated with these things. When there are, residents call and get immediate action. Not so in my neighborhood, where garbage collectors rarely pick up trash that spills as cans are emptied into the truck, where absentee landlords often stall on repairs and hide behind the threat of eviction should their tenants complain, where calls for code enforcement are put in a pile. In affluent neighborhoods, schools are well stocked with material resources and technology, and have the benefit of involved parents with disposable income and leisure time. Not so in my neighborhood, where the deteriorating school is short on many things, where parents often work multiple and seasonal jobs, where poverty, addiction and violence frame everyday life for the children. This simple act of visualizing the relationship that exists between specific institutions and the neighborhood, and determining the characteristics of that relationship, helps to outline transformational actions that may usher in shalom.

Influencing for shalom. How does this happen? In a couple of different ways. Obviously it happens when a church is present in a neighborhood. It happens even more when Christians in the institutions have a relationship with the neighborhood and can contribute to shalom through personal influence. For example, the Christian teacher who prays over every desk prior to her class arriving, Christian police officers who practice servant leadership as they relate with residents, Christian code enforcement staffers who believe the poor deserve protection from exploitative landlords, Christian TV reporters who feature stories of hope from the neighborhood—all have shalom influence.

But as we see in figure 3 on page 160, this also happens through strategic relationships *between institutions* in the different sectors. Beyond individual influence, we have the chance to influence how institutions relate to each other in a way that contributes to increasing measures of shalom. In my city, we realized that there were serious followers of Christ in law enforcement and education (public sector), business (private sector) as well as in the nonprofit sector. This led to the creation of an incredibly effective ministry that united those sectors in working toward shalom. Yet there are far simpler things we can do too.

Open your eyes! While the first, very practical thing we can do to understand our city is identify the ways institutions relate to neighborhoods and vice versa, the second is to observe. When we use simple observation techniques, we get a practical sense of the challenges and opportunities before us in the city.

Observation can take several forms. It can be as straightforward as counting the number of ethnic restaurants in a city, doing a "windshield survey" by driving around and observing the state of businesses in various neighborhoods or counting boarded-up houses in various parts of town. Those of us who participated in crafting the Lausanne Occasional Paper "Transformation of City Regions" have identified multiple things that can be done by basic observation and corresponding analysis to understand a city.[1]

Another type of observation uses an ethnographic approach. Intercultural expert Judith Lingenfelter encourages people who want to minister in a city simply to observe where people gather in a neighborhood and then interview residents. This accesses local knowledge about a neighborhood that can provide insight far beyond what an external observer could attain.[2] Concerning those interviews, Ray Bakke recommends posing a simple question to people: "What things do you think I ought to know about this neighborhood (or city/community)?"[3] This allows the residents to prioritize their responses, increases the authenticity of the conclusions we arrive at and allows us to observe through their eyes.

Dr. Mok Chan Wing Yan, a Hong Kong-based expert in crosscultural ministry among both urban and rural poor, suggests observing specific urban subcultures that often get overlooked, such as truck or taxi drivers, as a powerful way to understand and influence the city. Subcultures have their own diverse features. In one urban context Mok's team discovered one factor in the spread of AIDS. She placed medical data regarding the growth of the disease next to data about established trucking routes. Because prostitution tended to follow those routes, an indisputable link was established, and Mok's church members were able to work with the truckers to deal with this crisis, transforming the way cities along those routes dealt with the issue. In another city she discovered a huge gambling problem among taxi drivers, primarily due to the large amount of spare time on their hands. Her church was able to formulate a strategy to help taxi drivers deal with this problem and to reach them with the gospel.

Find out! We seek to know our city by *asking questions* about how our poorest neighborhoods experience key institutions in the various sectors. As we put on this *institutional* lens we can help to ensure that the strategies we pursue reflect real and felt needs. When we combine these with the *identity marker* lens, we can compile strategic questions that will help us frame an approach to building shalom in our city.

The following questions can help churches or groups use this process more systematically.

Onramp 1: Have your group ask these questions to get to know your city.

Using the *institutional sectors* lens, ask:

1. How many elementary-school neighborhoods exist in my city?

2. How many churches exist in my city? What neighborhoods do they fall in?

3. In the poorest of those neighborhoods, what are some things that characterize the way residents experience the school, various departments at City Hall (such as housing or code enforcement, city services, police), churches or social service agencies, local businesses, the media, and opportunities for work? What

opportunities exist to ask this question from inside the neighborhood?

4. If I were to list every Christian I know in this city and could chart their professions, what institutional sectors do they fall in? What sectors do I have a connection to or influence in?

5. To what extent does a dialogue exist in my city that has the potential to unite Christians across the sectors for transformational influence?

6. Are there specific ways in which political and business interests in the city have united to the benefit of a few without regard for those in the poorest neighborhoods?

Using a simple *observational* lens, ask:

1. In a single afternoon drive through my city, how many different ethnic restaurants can I count?

2. As I drive, do I notice that certain parts of my town are associated with various subcultures, such as goths, day laborers, skaters, yuppies, artists or gangs?

3. Is there an area of my city where businesses are boarded up or vacant? What geographic boundaries in my city define or surround those areas that are known as economically depressed?

4. Where do people go to recreate? Do all sections of my city have access to recreational facilities? Are the facilities of equal caliber?

5. Do certain parts of the city have major grocery stores while others do not? Do certain parts have a larger number of convenience stores?

6. Does one part of my city have a large number of check-cashing institutions but fewer banks?

7. What differences exist in the size, capacity and state of repair of the churches from neighborhood to neighborhood? How about the schools?

Using the *identity marker* lens, ask:

1. *Urbs* question: How many people live in my city? What's the ethnic breakdown of the population? Do certain ethnic groups tend to live in certain areas?

2. *Urbs* question: What geographic realities (for example, freeways, railroad tracks, housing stock, transportation systems) influence how people interact, or don't?

3. *Urbs* question: What percentage of the residents in my city can afford to purchase a median-priced home? What is the rental vacancy rate? Where do the poor live?

4. *Civitas* question: Does my city have a reputation? What is it known for? What events in the history of my city (good or bad) have contributed to this?

5. *Civitas* question: What kinds of things characterize the relationship in this city between (a) ethnic groups and (b) classes?

6. *Civitas* question: What civic associations, coalitions, networks or groups exercise the greatest influence in my city? Who are the key spokespersons for these?

7. *Anima* question: What kinds of things characterize the religious climate? What historical forces have contributed to this climate?

8. *Anima* question: What popular beliefs or assumptions tend to contribute most to people's behavior in my city? What misunderstandings of God most inform these?

9. *Anima* question: What perceptions about my city are prevalent from its residents? How does my city regard itself? Proudly? With

shame? With arrogance? With gratitude? What events in my city typify its self-perception?

TRANSFORMATIONAL ACTION #2: CONNECT YOUR CITY

When Catherine Franz finished her year of training in experiential discipleship as a resident of InterVarsity's Pink House Center for Urban Ministry Training in Fresno, her connections to ministries led to an amazing job: she is now director of Care Fresno, an innovative, award-winning program that unites churches, apartment owners, schools and the police in a public-private-nonprofit partnership that has transformed the experience of residents in dozens of what were the most marginalized neighborhoods of the city.

Here's how it happened. Police officers often lamented that they could drive drug dealers out of an apartment complex without having any positive impact; the dealers quickly reappeared. Leaders in a local faith-based nonprofit approached the police and the owners of apartment complexes that had high numbers of calls for service (such as 911 calls and requests for police) with an idea: Police would drive out drug dealers. Apartment owners would then set aside one or two units to be used for tutoring, afterschool programs, music lessons and other positive activities. And the faith-based nonprofit would recruit church folk to "staff" the sites. Then principals of elementary schools in the neighborhood of each complex became part of the discussion. Many responded positively by donating books, computers and software, as well as by assigning volunteer time from teachers to help create a holistic approach that integrated the school and home life of the children. The police would be more present and proactive, rather than simply appearing in a crisis.

This multisector strategy has proven to be transformational in measurable ways now for nearly ten years. In more than a dozen apartment complexes, the crime rate measured by calls for service to police has been reduced by an amazing 65 to 70 percent. Life for a number of Fresno's poorest residents is now characterized by a far greater measure of God's shalom; it's closer to the way things ought to be.

Sector connectors. Care Fresno is a good example of multi-sector collaboration, symbolized in figure 3. It works because Christ-motivated leaders are committed to more than personal witness, individual discipleship or private faith. They have found a way to integrate their commitment to Christ and their professional influence in the public sphere.

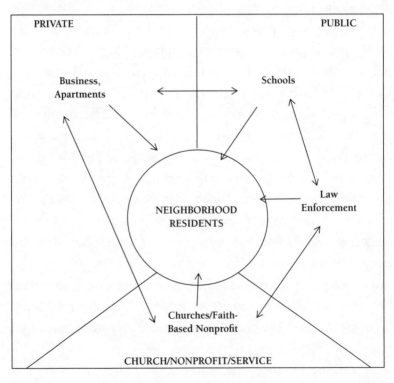

Figure 3

Given the problems that exist in many of the apartment complexes, Care Fresno workers realize that their professional influence alone will not be enough. For there to be real transformation, a more holistic, integrated approach is necessary. That requires multisector collaboration.

Whole city relational connections. How do initiatives such as this begin? Out of relationship. Care Fresno was inspired by city-focused Christians who began meeting monthly to consider the dramatic changes they saw taking place in the city, including out-of-control youth, huge increases in gang activity, ninety-three murders in a single year, unemployment at four times the national rate, a skyrocketing teen pregnancy rate, racism and lack of concern for the growing refugee population. The group, called No Name Fellowship, exists to mobilize God's people to address these challenges. It's eclectic, attracting individual Christians, business leaders, pastors, elected and appointed officials, and directors of missional agencies and nonprofits. Its purpose is to "release God's resources, through reconciled relationships, for the rebuilding of our city."

Focused associations. When Billy Graham came to Fresno in 2001 he remarked that it is "the most connected city in America." He was referring to how the Christian community works together intentionally on personal and institutional relationships. That intentionality is demonstrated in many ways. For example, in addition to the monthly No Name Fellowship gatherings, the directors of nonprofit, missional agencies meet for training, mutual encouragement and information sharing that specifically benefits that community. Called the City Builders Roundtable, this group is a lifeline for small nonprofits and has a profound effect on building and maintaining vision and increasing the capacities of these agencies to work for transformation.

The directors of ministries focused on at-risk youth gather separately to do the same. Called the ARMS Network (At Risk Ministries), this meeting attracts youth ministers, chaplains at juvenile hall and alternative-sentencing (boot-camp) personnel. They grapple with current trends, institutional challenges and personal obstacles faced when ministering to that population, transforming the way their work is done.

And finally, eight or so clusters of pastors meet monthly, representing more than a quarter of the churches in the city. These clusters are designated by geography (zip zones or natural boundaries). Pastors in each area meet to build relationships and discuss the forces shaping life there. These are different from traditional ministerial association meetings, which tend to exist to build collegiality alone. From the base of these clusters, pastors have designed mutual outreach events, have met with city leaders over justice issues and have confronted developers over plans that affect the community. They even have worked with other clusters to raise awareness in the faith community at large regarding the Fresno housing crisis and have sponsored events that united the city's entire Christian community.

Desperation and initiative. So, what does it take to create a climate of connection? First, in the case of Fresno, a climate of desperation created a context in which new collaborations could grow. No one entity or church felt it could begin to address the magnitude of the problems we all were seeing. Until a community achieves a consensus that systemic change must take place, no amount of meeting and eating together will be sufficient to unify God's people or to birth new strategies.

Second, it usually takes the initiative of one person who has earned the respect of the community and has visionary and relational skills, a person who can travel like a pollinating bee from church to church, agency to agency, civic leader to civic leader, creating a vision for the possible. This person must be supported by an institution that sees the merit in such activity, though in the short-term the institution itself will realize only a small measure of benefit.

Finally, for a citywide connectivity to be sustainable, it takes the initiative of young, emerging leaders to get involved at a grass-roots level and the development of a system of training and support for those leaders.

A climate of connection is crucial for real transformation to take place at a community level. Yet pastors, agency directors and other leaders are often so consumed with their own plans, their own sets of relationships and their own ministries that it's difficult to get them to raise their eyes from the immediate to see what's happening outside the circles of their normal responsibilities. In addition, there may be obstacles to collaboration in a city, such as racial divisions, denominational boundaries or unresolved historical conflicts. Power differentials between Christian ministries will stifle collaboration.[4]

There is little incentive to embrace the wider problems of the community when we are consumed with our own stuff. But if we create a relationship with someone outside those circles, suddenly we begin to care about the issues affecting their lives. We begin dreaming about ways we can accomplish our own ministry goals by the act of embracing the community's needs as a whole and mobilizing our people to be involved with others in meeting needs. The minute a real leader begins to sense the potential power of connecting their own people and their own ministry goals with the people and goals of other leaders, toward the end of accomplishing something larger and more comprehensive in the community, they decide to respond.

Onramp 2: Have your group ask these questions to connect your city.

1. What ministerial associations exist in our city? Who goes to them? Who doesn't go to them? What subject dominates discussion there? What person or church maintains the meetings, and how would they describe their momentum and their purpose?

2. What issues in our city create the greatest feeling of desperation on the part of the faith community?

3. What individual in the faith community of our city has broad respect across racial and ethnic lines and across denominations? Is there someone who is a natural bridge-builder, who is able to see the big picture of what's happening in the community and has the potential to attract and connect people to collaborative relationships? Would that person be open to brainstorming ways we could increase the connectivity of our city toward the goal of transformation?

4. What might be some ways for young, emerging leaders to grow their vision of a connected community and experiment with various forms of this? What roadblocks might hinder including young leaders in building citywide coalitions?

5. Can we identify individual churches and agencies in our city that are ministering separately in specific areas and whose approach could be made more holistic and transformational by uniting with other churches or agencies toward a specific goal?

6. What forum in our city is accessible to Christians in the private, public and service sectors where citywide issues can be discussed from a faith perspective and where God's people can be mobilized for action?

7. What are the greatest obstacles to collaboration that exist in this city?

8. What is one example in our city of a collaborative relationship built for the sake of transformation? How can it be replicated?

TRANSFORMATIONAL ACTION #3: SERVE YOUR CITY WISELY IN THE NAME OF CHRIST

Following the example of Jesus, who "came not to be served but to serve, and to give his life a ransom for many" (Mk 10:45), evangelical and mainline churches, missional organizations, parachurch ministries, denominations, and Christian colleges and universities recruit high school and college students every year to participate in short, intensive service or ministry projects in inner cities or urban neighborhoods across the United States. Hundreds of such service projects exist, involving thousands of students annually. Participants serve in soup kitchens, vacation Bible schools, neighborhood cleanups, painting projects, home repair and many other forms of hands-on help. They report that their experience in the city taught them valuable lessons about God, about their faith and about the city. They also often report that their help brought tangible encouragement to residents and even bore fruit for the gospel as children and families responded to Christ.

Without diminishing in any way the positive impact of these service opportunities, we must ask if they go far enough: "How did they contribute to *transformation* on a broader neighborhood or community level?" In asking this question I am in no way retreating from the belief that transformed people can transform society. Service that simply seeks to embody and demonstrate the love of Christ and calls for a response is central to the gospel. Such service is also transformational for those doing the serving. But in light of the dramatic changes taking place in cities today, we must ask if there is a way of *shaping* and *focusing* our service in the city in a manner that addresses and influences some of the larger forces at work there.

This is a call to serve our cities, but to go beyond one-time events, which tend to dole out individual doses of compassion. This is a call to serve wisely, shrewdly and in a way that contributes to the establishment of greater and greater measures of shalom. To accomplish that call, I invite you to use the following categories as a launching pad for further exploration. Ultimately you can use whatever influence you have to tailor your service in the city in the manner that best leads to the growth of shalom.

Service through suffering with. For most of us, serving someone means observing or hearing of a need and performing a compassionate action. But real compassion means something more. As mission writer Bryant Myers said, "Compassion requires that we go beyond seeing and hearing: we must be willing to feel."[5] The word *compassion* means to suffer with someone (*co* means alongside; *passion* means suffer, as in the passion of Christ).

This isn't easy for those of us in the West to embrace. I have observed, served and helped to send students to minister in some of the most horrendous urban settings in the world, including squatter settlements in megacities, scavenger communities in sprawling slums and inner-city neighborhoods that don't just look *like* war zones, they *are* war zones. In each of these communities my activist, can-do personality comes to the surface and I want to get to work designing programs and ways to serve that will make a difference. I want to *do* something. But I am often struck by how many people in those communities simply want me to sit with them, to know them, to see both their suffering and their joy and to know me as well.

Of my desire to always do something, Father Ben Beltran, who worked with the Manila scavenger community called Smokey Mountain, said,

> Randy, that's so American of you. You Americans have a saying, "Don't just sit there, do something!" But the people in my community would want to tell you, "Don't just do something, sit there!" First and foremost, they want to know if you are willing to sit with them, to be with them in their suffering. Will you take time to understand their suffering, its causes, its impact, your role in it, their role in it? Will you build a relationship, a partnership with them?

What meant the most to Smokey Mountain residents when our students came to live there was that the black flies covered their food too. The students did not insulate themselves from the people's problems. Of course, this is not to say that we are to be complacent about problems. It is all to say, first things first.

The implication of this is tremendous. For those of us who would design service opportunities in the city, it's not hard to jump right in, to organize work crews for a renovation project or to put on a Bible-themed carnival for children. But it takes creativity, discipline and patience to design ways to serve in the city that are built on the incarnational principle of sharing in people's suffering.

What might this look like? Perhaps it means that no matter what length the service project is, the very first component should include opportunities to listen to the stories of those we are serving and to share in their suffering. This should include visits to homes, meeting family members, sharing meals. It might be as simple but as significant as shouldering a portion of their story, what Melba Maggay calls the "restructuring of power relations."[6] We reject the identity of the outsider, refusing to come into a position of power by sweeping in with answers. We intentionally adopt a relational posture toward those we have come to serve, one that emphasizes solidarity and potential for partnership. In choosing this posture we are *not* saying that we bring nothing to the table. This kind of service simply says, "First suffer with; out of that shared suffering a partnership will grow." Tears first.

Service through holistic ministry. As I walked down an alley in one of the largest cities in the world, both sides of the alley were lined with teen girls dressed provocatively and making strong eye contact with passersby. The ministry director who accompanied me explained that this slum of more than a million people had four thousand teenage prostitutes with no prospects for other work, with no opportunity to go to school and with families in need of income.

I was overwhelmed with despair until he took me to his ministry's factory, several small rooms in the heart of the slum, where a handful of girls were assembling electronic equipment on one side and handicraft items on the other. The light of Christ and a clear and confident dignity shone on those girls' faces. What a contrast to the hollow expressions of those on the alley! Innologic is an innovative company/ministry designed to reach young prostitutes and preteen potential prostitutes through a holistic ministry of employment, church planting and counseling. It is transforming that corner of the slum by going beyond service, going beyond rescue work to create a self-sustaining, systemic change in that sector of the city that creates a pathway out of horror for young women and many others. The fact that the city was Calcutta and not Cleveland is irrelevant. With more than half a million child prostitutes in the United States today, every city needs an Innologic, or ministries like it that stress holistic solutions.

We have to see service in the city as a series of onramps that we provide for our friends and fellow church members. These onramps should provide an array of options for service, ranging from easy to difficult, from gentle to steep, so there is an entry point for each person's degree of readiness. A tutoring program is easy access; some of your participants will need that. Recruiting gang members into a job training program, walking alongside them through the process, finding them a job and mentoring them through their first year—as volunteers at Fresno's Hope Now for Youth do—has a more challenging incline. Some of your participants will be ready for that. But even the most challenging contexts for service offer easy access points. Some students sent to serve at Innologic went simply to befriend the girls and to organize fun activities for them. I have sent volunteers to Hope Now for Youth who simply organized a basketball tournament.

The point here is that while direct and individual acts of compassion and service are always appropriate, wise service in the city will attempt to link with and provide support to churches, agencies and ministries whose goal is the holistic transformation of the systems, realities and cycles that oppress residents and are obstacles to shalom. The most holistic ministries will still present a full range of entry points, from easier to more difficult.

Service in the new global city. Globalization is a complex, multifaceted, international phenomenon with major implications at multiple levels, both negative and positive, for cultures, economies, identity, health, the environment, religious faith and the mission of the church. Like it or not, it is the defining reality of this age, and we must ride with it, using it to benefit humankind, or be ridden over by it.[7] Cities are the driving force behind globalization, bypassing even nation-states in their level of connectedness; the new global urban marketplace is now the permanent infrastructure that holds the world together.[8]

How the process of globalization is understood and engaged in by
the church will fundamentally influence the church's existence, its
relevance in the world and the carrying out of its Great Commission
in cities.

Even those who do not view globalization from the perspective of
faith and who are positively inclined toward it recognize the potential
negative fallout of unrestrained globalization. Globalization expert
Thomas Friedman is concerned that many workers around the world
are oppressed by "unregulated capitalists, who move their manufac-
turing from country to country, constantly in search of those who will
work for the lowest wages and lowest standards." He has noted that
the two-fifths of the world currently living on less than a dollar a day
are unlikely to benefit from the opportunities in the new global marketplace.[9]

Economics. Now that the consumer is in charge, the global marketplace forces the lowest price possible, which often hurts workers. As
Friedman notes in his startling new book on globalization, *The World
Is Flat,* consumers say to companies, "'Give me more for less.' And
then companies turn to employees and say 'if we don't give them
more for less, we are in trouble. I can't guarantee you a job.'"[10] Man-
ufacturers outsource and send jobs offshore, and cities feel the impact immediately. Churches with real services to offer displaced
workers and agencies that anticipate the inevitable change by offering faith-based job retraining opportunities prime the pump for
transformation. Individual Christians who prepare inner-city children to take their place in a technology-driven economy give them
the skills they will need to benefit from a flat world—a world that
benefits those with access to technical and financial resources—and
not be flattened by it. The poorest 5 percent of the population has
only a 16-percent chance of achieving an average income.[11] A flat

world calls for a holistic church response.

The reality of globalization and its economic impact should influence how we facilitate service projects in cities. In his excellent book *To Live in Peace,* Mark Gornik cites economist William Julius Wilson's identification of "key problem areas for the inner city associated with the global economy: employment, training and wages."[12] As we design opportunities to serve, we can link to churches, agencies and ministries that serve those who have lost their jobs or migrants who have been attracted to new factories set up in cities just north of our southern border.

Culture. But the implications of globalization are more than economic. They are also cultural. Globalization facilitates religious and cultural pluralism in cities through migration, trade and increased interaction via technology. As we design opportunities to serve, we should link with ministries that know how to address the vulnerabilities experienced by those who are displaced. For instance, the predominant type of migrant in today's world is a young, unmarried woman.[13] In overcrowded cities, how would these young women best experience the love of Christ? As cultures collide within the pluralism of the new urban experience, is the church prepared to offer a welcoming place? We should link our service to ministries that consciously equip people for evangelism and ministry in religiously pluralistic environments, who know how to be, as Lesslie Newbigin said, "cultural pluralists without being religious pluralists."[14]

Marty and Joanie Martin are good examples of this in my neighborhood. After relocating to Lowell more than fifteen years ago, they have developed expertise in Hmong, Lao and Vietnamese culture that helps them communicate respect and friendship while openly naming the name of Jesus in all of the ways they serve. Marty is a pediatrician who gently communicates the love of Christ as he treats his neighbors and mentors Southeast Asian youth. As an artist, Joanie paints murals for the school and runs art camps for neighborhood kids. The love of Christ fills their home and they have provided many onramps for neighbors to experience a connection to Christians and to the church.

Youth. The implications of globalization for service in the city are more than economic and more than cultural; they are linked to technology and youth. As we design opportunities to serve in the city, we must recognize the power of the growing international youth culture being fostered by the Internet. Primarily an urban movement, "Techno-Culture," as author Sam George calls it,[15] knows no boundaries. It is tech savvy, youth oriented, linked in real time to the world and united by trends in pop culture. It uses the latest technologies not only for business but also as an essential tool in everyday life.

Our methods of serving must link with agencies and churches that "get" the tech pathway to the soul of youth. In Pasadena, California, Rudy Carrasco and the Harambee Family Center have set up a web-design program for teenagers from the neighborhood. Many of these kids have designed institutional websites for agencies and nonprofits. Tim Svoboda is taking that a step further in the huge city of Chennai (formerly Madras), India. He and his Youth With a Mission team have put together a Christian tech institute that trains Indian teens in computer-aided animation. They are assembling their own portfolios and seeing their lives transformed in the process. Tim's goal is that Chennai will be the Burbank of India.

Serving your city through specific forms of prayer. Mac Pier, director of Concerts of Prayer Greater New York, has noticed something amazing. In 1995, he and other concerned Christians began something called The Lord's Watch, a prayer meeting focused on New York City and patterned after the one hundred years of uninterrupted, twenty-four-hour prayer among Moravian Christians in the early eighteenth century. This updated version began with nearly forty-five churches and a thousand people. Each church took a day of the month, their people covering it twenty-four hours a day with prayers for the city in four areas: "revival in the church, reconciliation between races and denominations, reformation of society, and reaching the lost."[16]

The Lord's Watch continues, which in itself is a miracle. Yet even more is happening: Mac—and nearly everyone else—has noticed that, since 1995, New York City has experienced a 60-percent drop in its murder rate (from the 1990s), and it is now the safest large city of more than one million people in America.[17] The Lord's Watch model connects with a strong need young leaders consistently feel— that of uniting across denominational barriers to worship and pray together. The sense of unity created through global youth culture and music can be built on to include unity over the four areas that form the prayer of The Lord's Watch above. Every city needs a forum where average Christians can gain a vision for those four areas and can participate in the ancient call to "take no rest, / and give [God] no rest / until he establishes Jerusalem" (Is 62:6-7).

But cities also need places where leaders unite in prayer, seeking God to establish shalom in the streets. Pastors' Prayer Summits were born in the Pacific Northwest and have now helped invigorate unified prayer in cities across the country. Pastors come together for two days to seek God on behalf of their city, to build relationships and to care for one another spiritually. The first summit held in Fresno in 1992 led to a remarkable sense of resolve growing among Christian leaders that God's work in the city is paramount, not the reputation of any one ministry or church.

And specific ministries have grown out of these experiences. The

Reverend Roger Minassian attended a prayer summit immediately after the Los Angeles riots in 1992. After spending two days seeking God for his city, images of Los Angeles neighborhoods in flames began to overwhelm him. A key question burned into his soul: "What would cause a people to be so filled with despair that they would burn their own neighborhoods?" Placing himself in their shoes, he began to weep. (Because of his stoic personality, he can remember weeping only once before.) He knew God was telling him to act. Out of the prayer meeting and out of the tears, he formed How Now for Youth, which has gotten more than a thousand young men out of gangs and into jobs.[18] Serving your city by sponsoring a Pastors' Prayer Summit might be the most profound form of service you could perform.

Prayerwalking. But what if there was a way that you could pray spontaneously for your city, with little preparation or notice, using a mechanism that had the potential to bring transformation? What if this mechanism for prayer had the hidden benefit of getting you and your fellowship out onto the streets, helping you learn about your city by using your eyes and ears to search for clues to what God is doing and what he wants to do? Every year WayMakers publishes *Seek God for the City,* an amazing prayer guide designed to help churches or groups engage in what has become known as prayerwalking. This strategic practice is best defined as "praying on-site with insight."[19]

In Fresno, Pastor Jonathan Villalobos walks with a team of church members through the Lowell neighborhood, pausing to pray on street corners where there has been violence, in front of homes where he knows there to be domestic abuse, at the neighborhood school where he calls out children's names. Sometimes people ask what they are doing. He always responds by saying, "We are simply praying; is there something I can pray for you?" No one has ever said no. Some of these encounters have led to evangelistic conversations and to people coming to church. On one occasion the Lord led a team by an apartment complex where a young boy was trapped in the trunk of a car. It was 110 degrees that day, and his young playmates were unable to get him out. The team went to a nearby apartment to get some tools—and saved the boy's life.

The most dramatic experience of prayerwalking I've ever had came from a long-term prayerwalk. For over a year I prayerwalked weekly on one street in my neighborhood, past a pornographic bookstore. The presence of open pornography in the neighborhood was bad enough; children and college students alike were exposed to it every day. It drew an addicted and often illicit crowd. Other businesses suffered under its seedy influence. Worse yet, it was also across the street from a Christian men's recovery home, where men who had been addicted or recently in prison were trying to get their lives back together. God used that year of walking and praying to disturb me, to help me understand the consequences of this business's presence in the neighborhood.

I cried out to God over and over, for several months, to close it down. At some point in the year, that prayer became "Oh God, this business is twisting your image that you have placed in every woman and is contributing to the decline of this neighborhood. *Either close it down or burn it down.*" I prayed this prayer for months, until one day I reached that corner and stopped dead in my tracks. There the smoldering remains of that business lay like a black stain, burned to its foundation. Melted videocassette covers and charred, empty racks were the only remnants. My initial reaction was astonishment, even fear. Did I cause this? Was it even right that I prayed for this? Thankfully, there was no loss of life. At this writing, four years later, the lot is still empty.

Serving your city shrewdly. It has been said that one definition of madness is repeating an action over and over while each time expecting or hoping you will get a different, more desirable result. Rational people understand that if we want a different result, we need to change the action in some way. The church has been sending groups to do Bible clubs in inner-city neighborhoods, conducting city revivals and outreaches that make a splash, sending volunteers to serve in soup kitchens and food warehouses and handing out sandwiches. Many individual lives are certainly impacted by these acts of kindness. Yet the systems that generate a climate of chaotic youth, that generate spiritual hopelessness, that generate hunger and homelessness, are not addressed. We continue to dole out individual acts of kindness, hoping that it will somehow be transformational, yet we are surprised when the exact problems in the exact numbers appear again tomorrow.

Maggay tells the story of a journalist who asked Mother Teresa why she was merely responding to outward poverty instead of dealing with its real source, which was structural inequities between the rich and the poor. It was a good question, given that currently in our world "the richest 1 percent receive as much income as the poorest 57 percent."[20] Mother Teresa replied, "'That is a good idea. Why don't you do it?' As it was, she already had her hands full tending to the sick and sorrowing and dying."[21] This story helps me remember two things. First, direct acts of compassion are always called for. That is what Mother Teresa's life was about. In arguing for the kind of service in the city that goes beyond charity, I do not in any way want to disparage individual acts of compassion. But second, it's a reminder that some of us are called to take Mother Teresa's challenge to "go do it," to work for greater equity and the transformation of the systems.

By choosing forms of service in the city that cause us to suffer with those who suffer, we link our own well-being to theirs. We are not likely to give up soon or be satisfied with short-term influence if our own well-being is at stake. By choosing forms of service in the city that are holistic, we ensure that the root causes of injustice are addressed and that the help we bring is sustainable. By choosing forms of service that connect to the realities of globalization in the city, we ensure that the church is scratching where people are truly itching and that we are providing answers to questions that people are really asking and that we are proposing solutions to economic and social dilemmas that the world simply can't provide. And by choosing to serve our cities by orchestrating unified prayer for revival, reconciliation, restoration and reaching the lost, by helping Christian leaders unite in prayer over their cities and by getting members of our churches and fellowships onto the streets to pray "on-site with insight," we ensure that the transformation we seek is by the power of the Holy Spirit, not by our own.

If *knowing* our city and *connecting* our city requires asking some strategic questions, *serving* our city wisely and shrewdly does as well.

Onramp 3: Have your group ask these questions to serve your city wisely.

1. What church or ministry in our city is really in touch with people who are suffering as a result of poverty, addiction, exploitation, or the uncertainties and vulnerabilities brought on by migration or job loss? How might those ministries help to facilitate opportunities for members of my church or fellowship to "suffer with" and to listen to the most vulnerable in the city?

2. If my friends in church or on campus want to serve in the city, what options or pathways are usually presented? To what extent

do each of these opportunities focus on and contribute to holistic and systemic transformation in the community, that is, the growth of shalom (making things as they should be *for* people, *between* the people and *in* people)?

3. Who is knowledgeable about the major trends affecting life in our city, such as population growth, ethnic and cultural demographic changes taking place, shifts in the economy? Is there a process in my church that would link the resources and expertise of those sitting in the pew (for instance, in technology, banking, housing, conflict resolution) with the needs created by the great changes taking place in our city? What would it take to start that process? Who could we be in dialogue with over this?

Epilogue to Part 3

Bernard of Clairvaux, a contemporary of St. Francis of Assisi more than 850 years ago, captured the essence of what it means to be an authentic learner as well as the goal of authentic learning:

> There are those who seek knowledge for the sake of knowledge;
> That is curiosity.
>
> There are those who seek knowledge to be known by others;
> That is vanity.
>
> There are those who seek knowledge in order to serve; That is love.[1]

There is a reciprocal relationship between action and understanding. God has designed us in such a way that we don't fully know something until we have acted on it. And when we take action, especially in the form of service, it cements our understanding, sealing the truth in our souls and leading us to live out God's love.

This has been a book about how God can use ministry in the city as an onramp for our own growth in Christ and as an onramp to understanding the forces shaping life for the urban poor. It's been about how to use experience in the city in a way that assembles onramps of discovery for the friends we fellowship with—and how to do it constructively, without bringing harm to the city. And it's been about identifying transformational actions that disciples of Jesus can take as onramps to shalom.

THE THING ABOUT ONRAMPS

Onramps do one thing: they help you merge. They get you onto the freeway. What will it take to get God's people up to speed and moving in the same direction as God? The cities of the world are growing by more than one million people per week, and the most dramatic church growth is happening in the world's largest urban centers. Wealth and privilege are being consolidated into a shrinking number of corporate and individual hands while more than one billion people live in deplorable slums with little or no access to clean water or electricity. Yet we have a gospel that we know to be transformational, both for individuals and for communities. It seems clear what road God is on. That is the road I want to be on. That is the road I want to help my friends get on. For that, we need onramps.

HIGHWAY TO HEAVEN?

I stood sweating in the heart of a slum in one of the largest cities on earth. Calcutta is bursting with sixteen million of some of the poorest people on earth. I met families who had pieced together living spaces in that churning cauldron, "homes" of little more than a plastic tarp strung over sticks, many with entrances only three feet high. I could only imagine the heat under the black tarp.

Some of our group talked with an eighteen-year-old woman who was able to stand upright in her doorway, a luxury for this alleyway. Above and next to us a busy freeway roared, choked with traffic, the exhaust spilling down the embankment to her "house." She and her family of four lived in a six-by-eight-foot space. I was amazed to learn that she had been born in that very space herself, as were her two children. In at least two generations of her family's presence there, nothing had changed. There is still no electricity, no running water, no sanitation. Her husband's job only brings in enough for subsistence, not improvement. As we listened to her story through an interpreter, my eyes scanned the rest of the slum, passing over rusting corrugated tin, scrap metal and mile after mile of plastic. I saw families struggling to care for one another in an environment that was trying to kill them.

Because our position was slightly elevated, I could see to the edges of the community. On all four sides stood mosques, their minarets towering over the low dwelling places of the slum. Before I had a chance to reflect on this, we were surrounded by children. At first they were reserved and curious. But within five minutes, they were joking and laughing, climbing onto our backs, pulling us to their houses, holding our hands, tugging at our sleeves and generally being mischievous. They answered our questions in English and asked us some of their own. One little girl, Luma, reminded me of the kids in my own neighborhood. She was brash and confident, found everything funny and would not take no for an answer. Her bright eyes and wide smile radiated the image of God. When it was time to leave, we literally had to tear ourselves away.

That evening, the day's experience imprinted itself permanently on my life as I soaked in the luxury of a shower. No, I wasn't feeling guilty that I had access to running water and the families of the slum did not. What I was feeling was akin to amazement as I watched the dark grime from the slum pool at my feet. The children had been all over us, and I hadn't realized how I had been marked. In fact, it was impossible to be there and not be marked. My mind returned to those four mosques I'd seen and to the many churches in the neighborhoods of Fresno. Were they being marked? Was the reality of suffering there changing the way they saw their role? Or, somehow at night, like me, were they able to wash away the film and stay removed? What difference were the mosques making in the life of the woman standing in the doorway of her tiny, inadequate house, or to Luma, who would need more than a smile to fulfill her potential? The mosques had been there for years, yet conditions were not improved. The same goes for the church in many poor neighborhoods in the United States. We have been compassionate, have heard the cry of the suffering and have felt bad, but we have provided few models of community change, of the establishment of shalom.

Despite the vast difference between that slum and the Lowell community, my experience there taught me that they have many things in common. Poverty was handed down from generation to generation there. Same here. Children found ways to play and persevere, even in stark situations there. Same here. The slum was surrounded by religious institutions, while the physical degradation and injustice of the people's living conditions continued for decades. Same here. People there were spiritually hungry and open to relationships, to real communication, despite vast differences. Same here. For me, this experience was yet another onramp, an experience of Jesus inviting me to join him, to participate in deed, not only in word, in the good news of God's kingdom. It was a reminder that "those who know that God will wipe away all tears will not accept with resignation the tears of those who suffer and are oppressed now."[2] It was a summons to let myself stay marked.

The memory of Luma's bright eyes burning deeply into my own incites me to follow Jesus, who said, "I must proclaim the good news of the kingdom of God to the other cities also; for I was sent for this purpose" (Lk 4:43). The prophet Jeremiah said, "Seek the welfare of the city where I have sent you into exile, and pray to the LORD on its behalf, for in its welfare you will find your welfare" (Jer 29:7). Once again, I hear the Spirit of God saying, "Randy, get ready to merge!"

Epilogue

Experience in the city can be fertile ground for the planting and cultivation of something new—even something that grows in the cracks of a broken city sidewalk. Wildflowers have been known to split concrete. But experience—when unprocessed, uninterpreted, unapplied to a person's faith and unresponded to—can be confusing, debilitating or even empty. It can harden a person to the work of God. We must steward the urban experiences we help to orchestrate, see them as precious, as something that must not be wasted, leveraging them for God's shalom kingdom.

The lesson that blossomed for me the night the homeless man interrupted my small-group study of Isaiah 58 was hiding like a seed in the text: "If you offer your food to the hungry / and satisfy the needs of the afflicted, / then your light shall rise in the darkness / and your gloom be like the noonday. The LORD will guide you continually" (Is 58:10-11). It takes experience for the seed to germinate in me. I encounter God in the city, and he routinely helps me join in the flow of his work in the world.

As I write these words, twenty students are pouring into my living room. Tonight they will talk about what God is doing in this city and what their role might be in it. Tomorrow they will serve in the neighborhood and meet some amazing people. They will act, reflect and respond. I wonder what onramp will be created this time? For . . .

> A highway shall be there,
>> and it shall be called the Holy Way;
> the unclean shall not travel on it,
>> but it shall be for God's people;
>> no traveler, not even fools, shall go astray. . . .
> And the ransomed of the LORD shall return,
>> and come to Zion with singing;
> everlasting joy shall be upon their heads;
>> they shall obtain joy and gladness,
>> and sorrow and sighing shall flee away. (Is 35:8, 10)

Encounter God in the City Online Supplement

DRIVER'S ED: LEADER'S GUIDE TO DESIGNING
URBAN EXPERIENTIAL DISCIPLESHIP EVENTS

For more information on how to design, plan and lead your own experiential discipleship events in the city, see the online supplement. Go to ivpress.com and type in the title of this book.

There you'll find free bonus chapters and resources:

1. Dynamics of Growth Through Experience

2. Choreographing Experiential Discipleship in the City

Appendix A: Accumulated Wisdom from Urban Project Directors

Appendix B: Tools

Appendix C: Formats

Notes

Notes

Foreword
[1]Vincent J. Donovan, *Christianity Rediscovered* (Maryknoll, N.Y.: Orbis, 1983), p. viii.

Introduction
[1]Ray Bakke in *The Urban Face of Mission*, ed. Manuel Ortiz and Susan D. Baker (Phillipsburg, N.J.: P & R, 2002), p. 32.
[2]Bryant L. Myers, *Exploring World Mission: Context and Challenges* (Monrovia, Calif.: World Vision International, 2003), p. 72.
[3]Ibid., p. 72.
[4]"Centrifugal Forces," *The Economist*, July 16, 2005, p. 4.
[5]See the Lausanne World Forum publication "Towards the Transformation of Our Cities/ Regions," edited by Glenn Smith, Lausanne Occasional Paper no. 37 (Montreal: Lausanne Committee for World Evangelization and Christian Direction, 2005), which describes the city as a spiritually fertile place. I had the privilege of helping to write this document: <http:// community.gospelcom.net/lcwe/assets/LOP37_IG8.pdf>.
[6]"Centrifugal Forces," p. 6.

Chapter 1: Don't Bother Me. I'm Teaching on Compassion!
[1]The Brookings Institution, "Katrina's Window," 2005, <www.brookings.edu/metro/pubs/ 20051012_concentratedpoverty.htm>.
[2]See David A. Kolb, *Experiential Learning: Experience as the Source of Learning and Development* (Englewood Cliffs, N.J.: Prentice-Hall, 1984) for an explanation of "dissonance."
[3]Edgar S. Elliston and J. Timothy Kaufman, *Developing Leaders for Urban Ministries* (New York: Peter Lang, 1993), p. 95.
[4]Brian McLaren, *A Generous Orthodoxy* (Grand Rapids: Zondervan, 2004), p. 87.
[5]Jack Mezirow, *Transformative Dimensions of Adult Learning* (San Francisco: Jossey-Bass, 1991), p. 11.

Chapter 2: Disorientation and Discovery: Kundara and Peter
[1]For more on the role of reflection, see Pat Hutchings and Allen Wutzdorff, eds., "Knowing and Doing: Learning Through Experience," *New Directions for Teaching and Learning* 35 (San Francisco: Jossey-Bass, 1988), p. 35.
[2]Jack Mezirow, *Learning as Transformation* (San Francisco: Jossey-Bass, 1978), p. 22.

Chapter 3: Sandpaper Surprises and Reflective Learning: Napoleon
[1]Pat Hutchings and Allen Wutzdorff, eds., "Knowing and Doing: Learning Through Experience," *New Directions for Teaching and Learning* 35 (San Francisco: Jossey-Bass, 1988), p. 14.
[2]Jack Mezirow, *Learning as Transformation* (San Francisco: Jossey-Bass, 1978), p. 6.

Chapter 4: Action and Reflection: I Am Not Mr. Rogers
[1]See Michael J. Marquardt, *Action Learning in Action* (Palo Alto, Calif.: Davies-Black, 1999),
p. 133.

Chapter 6: Involuntary Peel: New Skin Stings
[1]Laurent Daloz, *Mentor: Guiding the Journey of Adult Learners* (San Francisco: Jossey-Bass,
1999), p. 23.
[2]Ibid., p. 23.
[3]Ibid., p. 133.
[4]Jack Mezirow, "Perspective Transformation," *Adult Education,* February 1978, pp. 100-110.

Chapter 7: The Smell of Shalom: Karly and Cassie
[1]Perry Yoder, *Shalom: The Bible's Word for Salvation, Justice, and Peace* (Nappanee, Ind.: Evangel,
1987), p. 11.
[2]Nicholas Wolterstorff, *Until Justice and Peace Embrace* (Grand Rapids: Eerdmans, 1983), p. 69.

Epilogue to Part 1
[1]Donald Schön, *The Reflective Practitioner* (New York: HarperCollins, 1983).

Chapter 8: Hidden Forces: Pay No Attention to the Man Behind the Curtain
[1]Melba Maggay, *Transforming Society* (Quezon City, Philippines: Institute for Studies in Asian
Church and Culture, 2004), p. 80.
[2]Robert Linthicum, *City of God, City of Satan* (Grand Rapids: Zondervan, 1991), pp. 40-79.
[3]Alfonso Weiland, *In Love with His Justice* (Lima: Asociación Paz y Esperanza, 2003), p. 13.
[4]Graham Gordon, *What If You Got Involved?* (Oxford: Paternoster, 2003), p. 49.

Chapter 9: Paul's Urban Tour: The Force of Identity
[1]*The Word in Life Study Bible* (Nashville: Thomas Nelson, 1996), p. 1990.
[2]*The Word in Life Study Bible* says Dionysius was a member of the council and Damaris was a
potential hetaira, a woman specially trained in philosophy who had access to men of position
and influence. See p. 1986.
[3]The Brookings Institution, "Katrina's Window," 2005, <www.brookings.edu/metro/pubs/
20051012_concentratedpoverty.htm>.
[4]Daniel Quinn, "Christian Athens," transcribed by Douglas J. Potter, *The Catholic Encyclopedia,*
2003, <www.newadvent.org/cathen/02043b.htm>.

Chapter 11: An Undetected Wave: The Force of Humanity in Motion
[1]V. T. Patil and P. R. Trivedi, *Migration, Refugees and Security in the 21st Century* (Delhi: Authors
Press, 2000), p. 178.
[2]Bryant L. Myers, *Exploring World Mission: Context and Challenges* (Monrovia: World Vision International, 2003), p. 37.
[3]Statistics in this paragraph are from Hans P. Johnson and Joseph M. Hayes, *The Central Valley*

at a Crossroads: Migration and Its Implications (San Francisco: Public Policy Institute of California, 2004), pp. 1, 7, 10, 48.

[4]Philip Jenkins, *The Next Christendom* (Oxford: Oxford University Press, 2002), p. 93.

[5]Ibid., p. 118.

[6]"Centrifugal Forces," *The Economist,* July 16, 2005, p. 4.

[7]Ellen Hanak and Mark Baldassare, eds., CA2025 report (San Francisco: Public Policy Institute of California, 2005), p. 25.

[8]Patil and Trivedi, *Migration, Refugees,* p. 166.

[9]Hernando de Soto, *The Mystery of Capital* (New York: Basic Books, 2000), pp. 79-82.

[10]Erla Swingle, "Cities," *National Geographic,* November 2002, p. 78.

[11]Ray Bakke, "Nature and Mission of the Church in the Urban World of Postcolonial Realities" class notes (Hong Kong: Bakke Graduate University, January 2002).

[12]Ray Bakke, "Nature and Mission of the Church in an Urban World" class notes (Kolkata, India: Bakke Graduate University, March 2004).

[13]Previous quotes from Neil Peirce, "Immigrants Wanted: Stalled Cities Beg for Vitality," *Fresno Bee,* May 16, 2004, p. F1.

[14]Randy Capps, citing 2005 Report on Immigration by The Urban Institute, as quoted in the *Seattle Times,* June 5, 2005.

[15]Dianne Solis and Ernesto Londono, *Dallas Morning News,* "Often Off the Books and in the Shadows, Immigrant Janitors Underpaid," January 5, 2004.

[16]Ray Bakke, "Nature and Mission" class notes, (Kolkata, March 2004).

Chapter 12: When Things Boil, Things Rise: Invisible Forces Revealed

[1]"Paul's Urban Strategy," *The Word in Life Study Bible* (Nashville: Thomas Nelson, 1993), p. 1977.

[2]John R. W. Stott, *The Message of Acts* (Downers Grove, Ill.: InterVarsity Press, 1990), p. 263.

[3]Ibid., p. 266.

Chapter 14: Hosea's Excruciating Assignment: The Riptide Force Away from God

[1]Derek Kidner, *The Message of Hosea* (Downers Grove, Ill.: InterVarsity Press, 1981), p. 12.

[2]J. L. Mays, cited in Kidner, *Message of Hosea,* p. 69.

[3]Kidner, *Message of Hosea,* p. 87.

[4]*New Revised Standard Version Reference Bible,* "Introduction to Hosea" (Grand Rapids: Zondervan, 1990), p. 1009.

[5]Kidner, *Message of Hosea,* p. 17.

Chapter 15: Race Matters: The Force of Racialization

[1]See Michael O. Emerson and Christian Smith, *Divided by Faith* (Oxford: Oxford University Press, 2000) for an exploration of individual versus systemic understanding of racism.

[2]Ibid., p. 7.

[3]David K. Shipler, *A Country of Strangers* (New York: Knopf, 1997), p. 564.

Chapter 16: So Many Choices: The Force of Pluralism

[1]Glenn Smith, ed., "Towards the Transformation of Our Cities/Regions," Lausanne Occasional Paper no. 37 (Montreal: Lausanne Committee for World Evangelization and Christian Direction, 2005), p. 29.

[2]Paul Swarup, "Conversion and the Gospel in a Pluralistic Society," *Transformation* 21, no. 1 (January 2004): 57.

[3]Lesslie Newbigin, quoted in Richard Tiplady, *One World or Many? The Impact of Globalisation on Mission* (Pasadena, Calif.: William Carey Library, 2003), p. 77.

Chapter 18: Personal Transformation That Leads to Community Transformation

[1]Os Guinness, *The Gravedigger File* (Downers Grove, Ill.: InterVarsity Press, 1983), p. 80.

[2]N. T. Wright, *Following Jesus: Biblical Reflections on Discipleship* (Grand Rapids: Eerdmans, 1994), p. ix.

[3]Jack Mezirow, *Transformative Dimensions of Adult Learning* (San Francisco: Jossey-Bass, 1991), p. 135.

[4]The turning point was the Lausanne Covenant, signed by evangelical leaders around the world in the 1970s.

[5]Melba Maggay, *Transforming Society* (Oxford: Regnum Books, 1994), p. 20.

[6]Quoted in Mezirow, *Transformative Dimensions*, p. 136.

[7]More of their story is detailed in Scott Bessenecker, *The New Friars* (Downers Grove, Ill.: IVP Books, 2006).

[8]For more information on InterVarsity's urban projects visit <www.intervarsity.org> and <www.fiful.org>.

[9]Richard Howell, "Transformation in Action" (given at the Forum for World Evangelization, Lausanne Committee on World Evangelization, October 2004), p. ix.

[10]Quoted in Eldin Villafañe, *Seek the Peace of the City* (Grand Rapids: Eerdmans, 1995), p. 3.

[11]Theologian Nicholas Wolterstorff is significantly responsible for this element of the definition.

[12]Perry Yoder, *Shalom: The Bible's Word for Salvation, Justice, and Peace* (Nappanee, Ind.: Evangel Publishing House, 1987), pp. 10-11.

[13]Ray Bakke, *A Theology as Big as the City* (Downers Grove, Ill.: InterVarsity Press, 1997), p. 192.

Chapter 19: Speed Bumps: Don't Misuse the City

[1]Hippocrates *Epidemics* 1.6.

[2]Duane Elmer, *Cross-Cultural Connections* (Downers Grove, Ill.: InterVarsity Press, 2002), p. 72.

[3]For a list of several simulations, visit Simulation Training Systems at <http://www.stsintl.com/schools-charities/>.

[4]Many other games or simulations accomplish similar things. Do an Internet search of "experiential learning" to get started. Intercultural Press is a good source for these: <www.interculturalpress.com>.

[5]John McKnight, *Building Communities from the Inside-Out* (Skokie, Ill.: ACTA Publications, 1997), p. 5.

[6]Ibid., p. 6.

[7]Michael Oleska, *Orthodox Alaska* (Crestwood, N.Y.: St. Valdimir's Seminary Press, 1998), p. 221.

Chapter 20: Three Transformational Actions

[1]Glenn Smith, ed., "Towards the Transformation of Our Cities/Regions," Lausanne Occasional Paper no. 37 (Montreal: Lausanne Committee for World Evangelization and Christian Direction, 2005). These include observing growth patterns, identifying sections or zones, seeing the social and economic patterns of neighborhoods, identifying power centers in the city, listing the felt needs of specific groups, being aware of traffic flow, determining how opinion and

news is spread, assessing whether people groups interact and how, locating ministries and churches, distinguishing between types of churches, asking about growth patterns of various churches, and gathering data on church plants or closures.

[2]Lingenfelter's ethnographic approach includes contacting the population, defining population divisions and characteristics, assessing population routines and opportunities for witness, learning the experiential and linguistic context for witness, analyzing social organization and leadership patterns, and analyzing values and features of the people's worldviews. Her practice is featured in Roger Greenway, ed., *Discipling the City* (Grand Rapids: Baker, 1992), p. 193. These are amazingly close to what we have recommended under the "identity markers" approach.

[3]Greenway, *Discipling the City*, p. 191.

[4]On this subject I recommend Robert Linthicum's *Transforming Power* (Downers Grove, Ill.: InterVarsity Press, 2003).

[5]Bryant L. Myers, *Exploring World Mission: Context and Challenges* (Monrovia, Calif.: World Vision International, 2003), p. 83.

[6]Melba Maggay, *Transforming Society* (Oxford: Regnum Books, 1994).

[7]Thomas L. Friedman, *The Lexus and the Olive Tree* (New York: Anchor Books/Random House, 2000).

[8]Saskia Sassen, *The Global City: New York, London, Tokyo* (Princeton: Princeton University Press, 1991), p. xxii.

[9]Friedman, *Lexus and the Olive Tree*, p. 207.

[10]Thomas Friedman, *The World Is Flat* (New York: Farrar, Straus and Giroux, 2005), p. 214.

[11]"Centrifugal Forces," *The Economist*, July 16, 2005, p. 4.

[12]Mark Gornik, *To Live in Peace: Biblical Faith and the Changing Inner City* (Grand Rapids: Eerdmans, 2002), p. 49.

[13]V. T. Patil and P. R. Trivedi, *Migration, Refugees and Security in the 21st Century* (Delhi: Authors Press, 2000), p. 166.

[14]Quoted in Richard Tiplady, ed., *One World or Many? The Impact of Globalisation on Mission* (Pasadena, Calif.: William Carey Library, 2003), p. 77.

[15]Ibid., p. 34.

[16]Mac Pier and Katie Sweeting, *The Power of a City at Prayer* (Downers Grove, Ill.: InterVarsity Press, 2002), p. 34.

[17]Ibid., p. 34.

[18]Roger Minassian's book, *Gangs to Jobs* (Lafayette, La.: Alpha Publishing, 2003), is the inspiring story of this process and the best handbook available for other cities wishing to start similar ministries.

[19]C. Peter Wagner, *Churches That Pray* (Ventura, Calif.: Regal, 1993), pp. 170-79.

[20]Myers, *Exploring World Mission*, p. 73.

[21]Maggay, *Transforming Society*, p. 69.

Epilogue to Part 3

[1]Quoted in Michael Frost and Alan Hirsch, *The Shaping of Things to Come: Innovation and Mission for the 21st-Century Church* (Peabody, Mass.: Hendrickson Publishers, 2003), p. 141.

[2]David J. Bosch, *Transforming Mission* (Maryknoll: Orbis, 2001), p. 400.

A man comes across an ancient enemy, beaten and left for dead. He lifts the wounded man onto the back of a donkey and takes him to an inn to tend to the man's recovery. Jesus tells this story and instructs those who are listening to "go and do likewise."

Likewise books explore a compassionate, active faith lived out in real time. When we're skeptical about the status quo, Likewise books challenge us to create culture responsibly. When we're confused about who we are and what we're supposed to be doing, Likewise books help us listen for God's voice. When we're discouraged by the troubled world we've inherited, Likewise books encourage us to hold onto hope.

In this life we will face challenges that demand our response. Likewise books face those challenges with us so we can act on faith.

LIKEWISE.   *Go and do.*